The Big Story

Take an express tour of the Bible

The Big Story

Big thanks go to Alex Shuttleworth and his incredible faith, to Rev. Richard Williams, Dr Michael Eldridge, Dr Viv Thomas and my Dad. Thanks again to Trevor Withers and Laurence Singlehurst for their patience and encouragement. The genesis of this project, as with so many things, is with Ailsa. May this guide help us all to live in the enormous, wondrous, generous story of God.

The Big Story was initially published in 2004 on a small print run. Many thanks to Cell UK for having the vision to take it to another level.

Printed by Stanley L. Hunt (Printers) Ltd., Rushden, Northants
Cover by bluepigdesign, Harlow, Essex based on an original idea by Alistair Bullen, ABA-design, Maidenhead, Berkshire

Pictures used by kind permission of Rydal Hanbury
www.rydalhanbury.com

First edition 2009

Published by:
Cell UK Ministries, Highfield Oval, Harpenden, Herts. AL5 4BX
Registered Charity No. 1088578

ISBN: 978-1-902144-41-2 E&OE

Contents

The Big Story

Not knowing this story would be like not knowing your own surname

Who doesn't love a good story? Stories are powerful. Great stories inspire and entertain us. News stories keep us connected to the wider world. Our own life-stories tell us who we are. Humans need stories like the air we breathe.

It should come as no surprise that when God chose to communicate with humanity, he chose stories. Jesus was a storyteller. 'There was a man who had two sons...' he began, and everyone listened. In fact, not only is the Bible packed with stories, the whole thing fits together as one massive story. So, whatever your background, you don't just have a life-story and a family tree, God has given you a big story that we're all part of – The Big Story. It's a story that tells us we're not here by accident, we're loved by Someone, called for a special purpose, destined for something wonderful. It is by far the greatest story ever told.

It's hard to express just how immense this story really is. If it's true - and there are many reasons for believing that it is – then it is *the* defining reality of your life. Not knowing it would be like not knowing your own surname.

There are, of course, other tales that compete for our attention: this week's headlines; this season's fashions; this year's sporting highlights; the latest movies, books and products; not to mention our own personal hopes and frustrations. There are lots of stories, but none like this. No other story makes sense of all the others. No other story brings love, hope and transformation like this one. No other story has a place for each one of us that will last forever.

What could be a better use of your time than this? Why not commit yourself to enter into this Bible story more deeply than ever before? The more you read, the more you'll see God at work in your life and in the world. In fact, the words of scripture are under a special kind of blessing. As you let their meaning shape your thinking and change your life, you'll begin to find your place in the Big Story. And you'll find that right alongside you is the main character himself, Jesus Christ. This is his promise: as we start to live in his story, he will come to live in ours.

How this guide works

The Big Story works through the whole Bible in eight episodes. In this guide you'll find an ***Overview*** of each episode, a list of the main ***Characters***, then fourteen ***Key Passages***. The chosen passages are probably the most significant ones in the whole Bible. They're short enough for regular reading, but also long enough to let the Bible speak for itself. Brief notes and questions have been added to help. Use the questions if you like (writing down answers may help you to reflect and learn) but don't worry if you can't think of an answer.

Through the Bible in 40 days

- Read the ***Overview***
- Read one of the ***Key Passages*** marked with a each day
- Consider the questions and pray

Through the Bible in 112 days

- As above, but read all fourteen ***Key Passages*** **-** one a day for 16 weeks. These tell the story more fully and shed light on each section by following up links in the Old and New Testaments

Meeting with a group or one-to-one

- At the end of each unit there is a brief plan for a ***Group Discussion***, and ***Questions for Reflection*** to use individually, one-to-one, or in a second group meeting.

Getting the Best out of Bible Reading

- Use a Bible that feels easy to handle and understand - for instance, Today's New International Version (TNIV), the New Living Translation (NLT) or the New Century Version (NCV). A clear copy of the world's bestseller is well worth the investment.
- The references in this guide (e.g., Exodus 33:1) refer first to the book of the Bible (in this case, Exodus), then the chapter (chapter 33) and then the verse (verse 1).
- If you can, find a quiet place to read and pray.
- Read regularly, daily if possible.
- Don't worry about what you *don't* understand – concentrate on living out what you *do* understand.
- Let the words of Scripture feed your soul. The purpose of Bible reading is not information-gathering but life-changing encounter with God. Like a love letter, its pages contain heartfelt communication from your Divine Pursuer. Like a spiritual map, you can truly find yourself in its vast compass. Like a great symphony, part of the point is just to let its music move you.
- There's no one way to read the Bible. The different questions provided illustrate various ways we can engage with God's word: meditating on it, imagining the events, reflecting on its meaning, turning it into prayer, and so on. But whenever God seems to be speaking directly to you, don't worry about the questions; just concentrate on what you hear.
- Let study lead to prayer. You may want to bear these questions in mind:
  - Is there something to thank God for?
  - Have I discovered something new?
  - Is there anything I need to repent of?
  - Is there anything I need to do?

Part of the point is just to let its music move you

The Big Story in a Nutshell

The Bible is the story of God, his world and us. It all springs from the desire in God's heart - his dream - which is to have people living in relationship with him on the world he created. These main characters - God, his people and the world - crop up at each stage of the story. At every point, human sinfulness threatens to ruin God's good plans; but at every point God intervenes to continue the story - his grace makes a way, the dream will not be defeated.

There are lots of ways to tell the story of the Bible. In fact, at several points God's people have taken time to set out the big picture (for example, Joshua 24:1-15, Nehemiah 9, Psalm 105, Acts 7, Acts 13:16-39 and Hebrews 11). This guide focuses on the eight major episodes of biblical history. Some episodes develop over the course of many generations; in others the action unfolds in just a few days. But together these eight episodes take us through the whole story of scripture.

The Big Story begins with **Creation and Fall**. God created the world, and then he made humans with a unique purpose - to know him and to govern his creation. The fall came when selfish humans, following the lead of Adam and Eve, rebelled against their Creator.

Despite all this, God decided to bring his broken creation back to himself, starting with **The Chosen People**. He chose Abraham and his descendants to be the ones who would know his blessing and learn his ways. When Abraham's descendants, the Israelites, found themselves as slaves in Egypt, God sent Moses to save them and bring them into **The Promised Land**. Here, as at the beginning, they were called to know him and be a picture of his plans for the world. But once again this never fully happened. Israel continued to rebel against God, and eventually he judged them in the form of **Exile and Return**. Half the nation was deported by Assyria and then the other half was captured by the Babylonians. But God still would not give up. He bought some Israelites back to rebuild Jerusalem and to wait for God's great purpose to be fulfilled.

At that time, God sent his own Son to complete the story. Jesus called this **The Kingdom of God.** He started to set right all that had gone wrong since the beginning: he healed the sick, offered forgiveness, and called a new family of disciples to follow in his ways. But setting things right would cost more than that. Jesus knew that only if he suffered a rebel's death on the cross would God's rebellious people go free. **The Cross of Christ** is at the heart of the Bible story. Because of this, the story could continue with the **Resurrection and the Church**. God raised Jesus from the dead as a sign that sin and death will not have the last word. God's unstoppable life is now at work in the church. God sent his Holy Spirit so that we could live as his people were always meant to live and spread the good news of Jesus around the world.

Finally, Jesus now reigns with the Father until he finishes his work in **The New Creation**. One day all humankind will face judgement, but God will save his people and bring them to live with him in a renewed creation. At last, God's people and His world will be gloriously completed and finally restored. The purpose of creation will be fulfilled, the dream made real, God's persistent love triumphant. End of story.

At every point we threaten to ruin the story, but God intervenes

	Episode	Through the Bible	Summary	Main Characters
1	Creation and Fall	Genesis 1-11	God created the universe and gave humans a special role, but sin has spoiled God's world	Adam & Eve, Noah
2	The Chosen People	Genesis 12 - Deuteronomy	God chose Abraham as the father of the Jewish people, then rescued them from Egypt	Abraham & Sarah, Isaac, Jacob, Joseph, Moses
3	The Promised Land	Joshua - 2 Chronicles	God gave his people the land of Israel and then kings to lead them, but many disobeyed him	Joshua, Samuel, David, Solomon, Elijah, Elisha
4	Exile and Return	Ezra - Malachi	Israel was split into two: one kingdom was destroyed, the other was exiled in Babylon and eventually returned	Jeremiah, Daniel, Ezra, Nehemiah
5	The Kingdom of God	The gospels: part I	Jesus announced God's kingdom, worked miracles and called disciples	John the Baptist, Mary, Jesus, the disciples
6	The Cross of Christ	The gospels: part II	Jesus died in our place and suffered the cost of setting the world to rights	Jesus
7	Resurrection and the Church	The gospels: part III, Acts-Revelation 20	Jesus rose from the dead, ascended to heaven and sent the Holy Spirit on the church	Peter, Paul & the early church
8	The New Creation	Revelation 21-22	Jesus will return to complete the new creation and God's people will live with him forever	

Bible Timeline

1 Creation and Fall

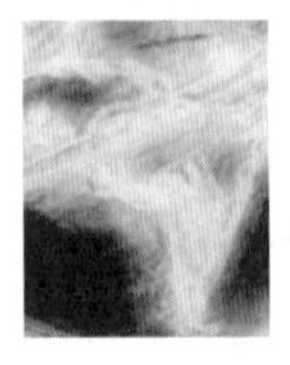

2 The Chosen People

3 The Promised Land

4 Exile and Return

TIME	EVENT
Unknown	Creation Adam & Eve The flood
1800 BC?	Abraham & Sarah travel to Canaan
	Isaac Jacob & his family (the 12 tribes) Joseph
1300 BC?	Moses The exodus Joshua Conquest of the promised land
	Israel ruled by judges
	King Saul
1000 BC	King David King Solomon
930 BC	Northern kingdom (Israel) splits from Southern kingdom (Judah)
722 BC	N. Israel invaded by Assyria
597 & 587 BC	Judah exiled in Babylon
538 BC	Exiles return to rebuild Jerusalem

BETWEEN THE TESTAMENTS	
539-330BC	Judah under Persian rule
330-166BC	Judah under Greek rule
166-63BC	Revolution & independence
63 BC onwards	Judah under Roman rule

5 The Kingdom of God

6 The Cross of Christ

7 Resurrection and the Church

8 New Creation

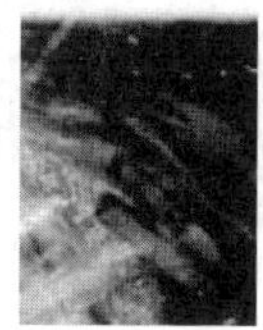

TIME	EVENT
4 BC?	Birth of Jesus
	Baptism & temptation
	Ministry around Galilee
30 AD	Entry into Jerusalem Last Supper, arrest, trial & crucifixion
	Jesus appears to the disciples
	The ascension
	Holy Spirit comes at Pentecost
	Early church in Jerusalem
	Gentiles join the church
34 AD?	Paul converted
45-60 AD	Paul's missionary journeys
70 AD	Destruction of Jerusalem
50-90 AD	New Testament books written
unknown	Jesus returns to judge all people
	A new heavens and a new earth

Episode 1

Creation and Fall

GENESIS 1-11

Overview

Genesis means 'beginnings'. The first chapters of Genesis tell the story of creation and try to explain why things are the way they are. What makes humans different to other animals? Why do we have families? Why is the world so beautiful and yet so broken? After its opening account of creation (Gen 1:1-2:4) Genesis follows the story of the earliest humans. Despite being given great privilege and responsibility, Adam and Eve disobey God's command and are thrown out of the Garden of Eden (Gen 2-3). Their descendants, beginning with Cain and Abel, get caught in a spiral of jealousy, violence, revenge and abuse (Gen 4-5). This comes to a head in the time of Noah with God's judgement in the form of a flood (Gen 6-9). God saves Noah's family and every species of animal, and he promises never again to wipe out life on the earth. So the spread of humanity continues (Gen 10), but so does our selfishness and arrogance, for example at the Tower of Babel (Gen 11).

It's easy to get side-tracked into worrying about the early chapters Genesis - Was the world made in 7 days? Did people once live for hundreds of years? These chapters weren't written to answer those questions. They were written to set the record straight about who made the world and how we are to live in it. Many people believed then (as some do now) that the universe is basically in chaos with many different powers or 'gods' in charge. Genesis tells a different story. It teaches that one God made the universe, according to his own plan, and what he made was good. Evil doesn't belong in God's world; it's an intruder which has flourished because of human disobedience.

These chapters were written to set the record straight

So, despite all its wonder and goodness, the first episode of our story is basically a tragedy. Humans are unique - made in God's image to worship him, love each other and care for creation. But we have squandered our potential. From the beginning, human families and societies have turned away from God and his wise plans for creation. This is sin - the blight on every life, the dark side of every human action, and the root cause of all the death and destruction around our world. The beauty of creation is a sign of

Can you see, in our world, the effects of the judgements God gave (v. 14-19)?

Genesis 6 The flood

This passage draws us back to the dawn of humanity and a terrible grief in the heart of God at the wickedness in the world (v. 6). Somehow he must act against evil, and yet he also desires to save.

What qualities does God display in this chapter?

What does the flood story show about the seriousness of sin?

Genesis 8:13-9:17 God's covenant with creation

This is the first covenant (agreement) in the Bible. Noah plays a mediator role – he receives the promise (see 6:18) and therefore its blessings come to others through him. Notice that this covenant is accompanied by a sacrifice (8:20) and a sign (a rainbow).

Covenant	Mediator	Promise	Conditions
Between God & all creation	*Noah*	*Not to flood the earth again (Gen 9)*	*None*

How does God make allowances for human sin in this passage?

How is Noah's experience of being saved like being a Christian?

OLD TESTAMENT LINKS

Psalm 8 Our place in the universe

We often feel so small in the universe – just as the Psalm says (v. 3-4). But God has great plans for us and an awesome destiny that hasn't changed. We don't deserve this wonderful role, but eventually God sent Jesus to take it on our behalf – and one day we will share it with him (see 2 Timothy 2:12).

What is our place in the universe, according to this psalm?

How does it feel to know that this is what God made you for?

Psalm 19 God's glory and revelation

According to this psalm, God is revealed in both his creative work and in his written word (recorded for us in the Bible). Both come from God, both are good, and both help us see his glory, if we're willing to look.

What do the skies tell you about God?

God's blessing, but its brokenness is a sign of God's judgement and of a runaway world left to its own devices.

And yet, even in these early chapters, we also catch a glimpse of God's boundless grace. He created us in love with the freedom to respond to him. He refused to give up on Adam and Eve, or their descendants. Even now, he sustains the world and gives us life and every good gift. Though he has every right to disown us, instead he has committed himself to the slow and painful task of redeeming creation at all costs.

Characters

Adam and Eve: Genesis 2-3
Cain and Abel: Genesis 4
Noah: Genesis 6-9

Key Passages

Genesis 1:1-2:4 Creation and the image of God

In this majestic and poetic opening sequence, God creates everything by his choice and in good order. At first, creation is 'formless and empty' (verse 2). Then, in days 1-3, God establishes the form (day/night, sky/sea, land/seas); and in days 4-6 he fills the emptiness (lights for the day/night, creatures for the sky/sea, creatures for the land). The crown of the whole process is humanity, made in God's image to know him and rule creation on his behalf (1:26).

What kind of God comes across in this passage?

What signs of order and goodness in creation can you thank God for?

Genesis 2:4-25 Relationships and family

This account covers similar ground to Genesis 1 but in story form. The name Adam means 'humanity'- so in this passage we see a picture of God's intentions for every one of us. We are made for a special relationship with God (v. 7), to care for the world (v. 15) and to love each other (v. 18).

What is special about Adam, about Eve, and about their relationship?

What does God give in this passage? What does he ask for?

Genesis 3 The fall and God's judgement

This is the turning point in the story of Adam and Eve and of humanity. It's hard to pinpoint when it might have occurred in early history. It's much easier, and more important, to see how it plays out in each of our lives.

What do you notice in this passage about the causes and effects of sin?

What is your attitude to the scriptures and the Big Story they contain? How does it compare to this psalm?

Psalm 51 A sinner's prayer

Just about everyone who has ever lived has repeated Adam and Eve's disobedience in their own way. Here King David faces up to his own sins of adultery and murder (see 2 Samuel 11-12).

What has David learnt about sin?

Why not use this prayer now and confess anything that comes to light?

Psalm 104 God and his creation

Notice how this Psalm praises God for every part of his creation: the environment, work, food…and wine (v. 15)! As the apostle Paul said, 'everything God created is good, and nothing is to be rejected if it is received with thanksgiving' (1 Timothy 4:4).

What is there in your life and environment to praise God for?

Song of Songs 6 Sex and celebration

Somehow this graphic, stirring love poem made it into the Bible! Perhaps God is not as ashamed of sex and romance as some might think. After all, they are part of his good creation, to be enjoyed in faithful marriage and honoured by others (like the friends in verses 1, 10 & 13).

How do you react to this love poem?

What does it show about true love?

NEW TESTAMENT LINKS

Matthew 19:1-12 Marriage

See how Jesus lives in the story of the Old Testament. The words of Genesis shape his thinking on the covenant of marriage, but he's also able to see how the earlier episodes of God's story (like Moses' divorce laws) can be developed by what comes later.

What does it mean today for us to respect the special value of marriage?

Romans 1:18-32 The story of sin

Paul is explaining that nobody, not even God's people, has escaped the corrosive power of sin in a fallen world. To do this he tells here a kind of

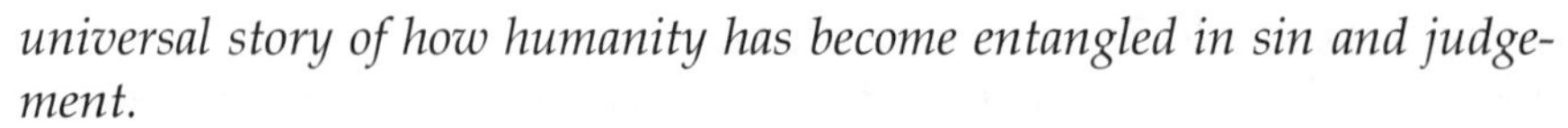
universal story of how humanity has become entangled in sin and judgement.

Can you see the opening chapters of Genesis in this passage?

Can you see our modern world in this passage?

Romans 5:12-21 The second Adam

In this complicated passage Paul compares the effects of two lives: Adam and Jesus Christ. Adam's sin ruined the world, but Jesus' obedience started to set it right. Humans still sin and die, just as Adam did. But thanks to Jesus we can be forgiven and rise again after death, just as he did.

Take a close look at Paul's reasoning. What did Adam bring into the world?

What has Christ brought into the world?

Revelation 22:1-5 The garden and the city

This final vision of the new creation reminds us of the Garden of Eden. But it also pictures the completion of all that Eden was meant to be. Only God can bring this future to pass, but the Bible also challenges us to bring a taste of heaven to earth (as we say in the Lord's Prayer).

How does this vision echo the Garden of Eden?

How can you turn these words into prayer for the world?

Creation and Fall: Group Discussion
Study Passage: Genesis 1:1-2:4

What strikes you from this passage?

What deep truths about creation do you think this passage illustrates?

What role do humans have? How does sin corrupt this role?

This passage speaks of the power of creativity and of rest. What does it mean for you, where you are, to be creative and also to rest?

Questions for Reflection
How has God been speaking to you about himself and the Big Story?

What has challenged or inspired you?

The first episode of the Big Story concerns a beautiful and abundant creation, the tragic brokenness of sin, and God's faithful desire to complete what he has begun.
How can you see these themes playing out in your life?

Episode 2
The Chosen People
GENESIS 12 – DEUTERONOMY

Overview

Episode 1 of The Big Story ended in catastrophe with nothing but the promise of God to give us hope. We might expect God to come up with some large-scale solution to redeem creation, but instead he starts with one man. Why did God choose Abraham? No one knows, except that he had to start somewhere!

Episode 2 takes us right back to this slow and distant beginning in the ancient tale of one man and his family. God chooses a people and binds himself to them with a solemn covenant. God promises Abraham many descendants, a land for them to live in, and that Abraham will somehow be a blessing to the rest of the world. His son Isaac and grandson Jacob receive these promises, too. Genesis chapters 12-50 follow the twists and turns of this family's story and end with Jacob's 12 sons in Egypt having been saved by the young dreamer, Joseph.

Why did God choose Abraham? He had to start somewhere!

Centuries go by, and Jacob's sons have developed into 12 tribes, but they live as slaves in Egypt. God calls Moses to lead them in an exodus - an escape from Egypt and into a land of their own. The books of Exodus and Numbers follow this great journey: a miraculous departure from Egypt, the crossing of the Red Sea and God's provision in the wilderness. Despite all this, the Israelites are often far from what God had called them to be. At times they grumble, they turn back to other gods and even refuse to risk entering the Promised Land. How can God fulfil his promises to Abraham through these stubborn descendants? And yet God remains committed to his people.

Over all this time, God gives the Israelites more than just their freedom. From the beginning he reveals himself to them. This includes giving the gift of the law, which enables them to please God in the land he would give them (much of this law is in Leviticus and Deuteronomy). Most wonderfully of all, God gives Israel his presence with them. This is shown through miraculous signs, a divine throne (the Ark of the Covenant), and a holy place (the Tabernacle). It is here, at the Tabernacle, that priests would organise sacrifices and offerings to God. Offering food and animals to God was an imperfect way of worshipping him, but it reminded Israel that a holy God can't live with an unholy people unless some cost is borne and their sins are somehow dealt with.

Characters

Abraham: his prayer (Genesis 18); the sacrifice of Isaac (Genesis 22)
Isaac: Gen 21-35
Jacob: Jacob and Esau (Genesis 25); Jacob's dream (Genesis 28); wrestling with God (Genesis 32)
Joseph: his dreams (Genesis 37); God's wonderful deliverance (Genesis 45)
Moses: his birth (Exodus 2); his call (Exodus 3); crossing the sea (Exodus 14); seeing God's glory (Exodus 34)

Key Passages

🚌 Genesis 12:1-9 Abraham chosen for blessing

Here is a true highpoint in the Bible. In a world of curses and judgement God begins the long road back to redemption. A hint of Eden returns in these gracious promises, and the seed of faith is planted in the heart of one man.

Enter this passage through your imagination. How do you think Abram might have felt?

How might God might be calling you, and what might need to be left behind?

Genesis 17:1-16 New names and circumcision

Covenant	Mediator	Promise	Conditions
Between God & all creation	*Noah*	*Not to flood the earth again (Gen 9)*	*None*
Between God & Abraham's family	*Abraham*	*A nation of descendants and a land for them (Gen 12, 15, 17)*	*Circumcision*

God is a personal God. He commits himself to his people and wants them to commit to him. Here he sets out his covenant relationship with Abram (renamed 'Abraham'): God promises a land and descendants; Abraham promises to circumcise his male descendants.

What signs are there in this passage that God and Abram are bound to each other?

Genesis 32:22-32 Jacob wrestles with God

Jacob is about to meet his brother Esau, whose birthright he stole. Up to this point, Jacob has prospered mostly by deception and trickery, but here he finally meets his match. In this mysterious encounter he comes up against a God who brings him to the end of himself. Once again, God confers a destiny by giving a new name: Israel. Together, ten of Jacob's sons (plus 2 grandchildren) would become the 12 tribes of Israel.

What strikes you from this passage?

Have you ever wrestled with God? Why does he allow us to do this?

Exodus 2:23-3:22 Moses is called by the LORD

Hundreds of years later, God's promise of descendants to Abraham has been fulfilled but they are slaves in Egypt. God appears to Moses and gives him a name to use ('I am' or, in Hebrew, Yahweh - v. 14-15 – sometimes shown in Bibles as 'the LORD'). This is not just one god among many, or even 'God' in general, this is the LORD, the 'I am', the God of the universe who takes a unique interest in Abraham's descendants.

What does God reveal about himself through this encounter?

Exodus 12:1-16, 29-42 The Passover

The plague on the firstborn is the last of 10 plagues, which were God's judgement on Pharaoh, Egypt's arrogant ruler. But the Israelites aren't just to assume they are safe - God's people need his protection, here in the form of the blood of a spotless lamb.

What details of the death of Jesus can you see foreshadowed here?

Exodus 13:17-14:31 Crossing the Sea

The momentous events of exodus would forever remain the foundation of Israel's identity. We see here once again that it is God who provides salvation for his people, who often contribute little but their own helplessness.
How does God show his care for the Israelites in these events?

Exodus 20:1-21 The Ten Commandments

Covenant	Mediator	Promise	Conditions
Between God & all creation	*Noah*	*Not to flood the earth again (Gen 9)*	*None*
Between God & Abraham's family	*Abraham*	*A nation of descendants and a land for them (Gen 12, 15, 17)*	*Circumcision*
Between God & Israel	*Moses*	*Blessings in the Promised Land (Exodus 19-24)*	*Obedience to God's law*

Having rescued his people, God sets boundaries for them to live within. In each case, the command is there not to restrict life but to protect it, and to safeguard the goodness of the things God has given us. The Ten Commandments form part of a detailed covenant made at Mount Sinai, where God said 'I carried you on eagles wings and brought you to myself. Now if you obey me fully and keep my covenant, then out of all nations you will be my treasured possession' (19:4-5). As with other covenants it was accompanied by sacrifice (24:5) and a sign (sprinkled blood – 24:8).
What reasons does the LORD God give for following some of the commandments?

What does it mean for you to walk in these commandments?

Exodus 33:1-4; 33:12-23, 34:4-7 Moses intercedes and sees God's glory

In a shocking display of rebellion, Israel turned away from the LORD to a god of their own making (Exodus 32). Here all God's plans for Israel hinge on his relationship with Moses (see 32:10). In these encounters we catch a glimpse of the heart of God and of the personal, responsive relationship he wants to have with us through prayer.

What do these events reveal about God?

What is your response to this God?

Leviticus 16:1-22 A day to atone for sin

Leviticus provides details of Israel's developing religious life, including the Most Holy Place – a sacred tent where God dwelt with his people. But even Aaron, the High Priest, could not regularly approach the Most Holy Place. Only once a year can he make atonement for himself and for Israel. Atonement brings God and his people back together. The sacrificial blood, and the scapegoat (v. 20-22), were a sign that atonement can never happen without cost.

How does this ceremony illustrate the seriousness of sin?

What keeps us from grasping the gravity of sin in God's eyes?

Numbers 13:1-2, 13:26-14:4, 14:20-25 Rebellion
Even on the verge of Canaan, God's faithfulness to his people doesn't find a trusting response. And so entry into the promised land was delayed by a whole generation.
What keeps God's people back from the promised land?

What would it mean for you to have the spirit of Caleb (14:24)? Why not ask God for this now?

Deuteronomy 6 Remembering God
Deuteronomy takes the form of Moses' great farewell speech. God would finally bring the Israelites into the Promised Land, but once there they would be responsible for living the way God intended. The choice to follow

God or not would make the difference between blessing and curse (verses 13-14, see Deuteronomy 28). Verses 4-5 became a daily Jewish prayer (called The Shema).
Why should Israel remember God?

What makes us forget what God has done for us? How can you avoid this?

NEW TESTAMENT LINKS
Matthew 1:1-17 Abraham's Line
Matthew can think of no better way to start his gospel than with the family tree of Abraham. Notice some of the names on the list: Isaac and Jacob (v. 2)...King David and Solomon (v. 6)...and finally Jesus Christ (v. 16). God truly did bring blessing to the nations through Abraham – through the story of his family, recorded in the Old Testament, and through his greatest descendant: Jesus himself.
Can you see what an immense plan God put into operation through Abraham's family?

There is a place in Jesus' family tree for all kinds of people; in fact, for anyone who believes in him ('Jesus is not ashamed to call them brothers and sisters' Hebrews 2:11, see Romans 4:16-17). That means there's a place for us, too. How does this encourage you?

Matthew 5:17-30 Jesus fulfils Israel's law

Here Jesus stands, like Moses, 'on a mountainside' (5:1) and teaches people how to truly fulfil God's commands. Jesus had immense respect for the law, but he also knew that the change in people's hearts must go deeper than simply following rules and regulations. In some ways Christians are free from certain Old Testament laws (for instance, about sacrifices or forbidden foods) but God's purpose remains – that we should please him by living as we were made to live.

How can you act on Jesus' instructions here?

Hebrews 11 Faith in God's future

The book of Hebrews was written to encourage Christians to persevere like the great characters of the Old Testament. We are all part of the same story, and somehow we need each other (v. 39-40). Our walk with God will only flourish with the faith they displayed; their story only makes sense because it points to the greater reality we now experience in Christ.

Which example of faith sticks out for you and how can you follow it?

The Chosen People: Group Discussion

Study Passage: Genesis 12:1-9

What strikes you from this passage?

What seeds of the rest of the Bible story can you see in these verses?

What was the cost to Abraham of following God?

What has God called you away from? What is he calling you to?

Questions for Reflection

How has God been speaking to you about himself and the Big Story?

What has challenged or inspired you?

The second episode of the Big Story is about being chosen by God, given great covenant promises and called to obey him.
How can you see these themes playing out in your life?

Episode 3

The Promised Land

JOSHUA – 2 CHRONICLES

Overview

Out of nothing, creation; then out of nothing, a nation. By the end of Deuteronomy God has almost fulfilled his promise. Against all odds Abraham's descendants find themselves on the verge of a land of their own, a land of plenty where they can know God's blessing. The book of Joshua recounts how he leads Israel to occupy the land and defeat its inhabitants. In a broken world, the only way to establish a nation and make a clean break from the godlessness of local cultures was through military force. This was a terrible cost, but it would bear fruit if Israel could keep the truth about God alive and become a sign to the world of his good plans. The only question is: would they?

Once they enter the promised land, Israel's tribes are at first united by a series of judges who deliver them from foreign oppression (see the book of Judges). Eventually, though, they ask Samuel - the last of the judges - to appoint a king to rule them. The first king, Saul, succeeds as a warrior but fails to follow God wholeheartedly. And so Samuel anoints David as his successor. Despite Saul's jealous rage, David prospers and eventually becomes established as Israel's king (see 1 & 2 Samuel).

Against all odds they find themselves on the verge of a land of their own

David's life is far from perfect, but there's no doubt where his heart lies. He never forgets to rely on his God, as many of the Psalms bear witness. And God makes a covenant with David: he promises that David's royal dynasty will continue forever and one day rule the whole earth. David's son Solomon later builds a lavish Temple for the Lord, and in this way the national history of Israel comes to a climax - safety, wise rule, and the presence of God in his Temple.

But this brief golden age doesn't last. Despite his wisdom, Solomon enslaves many Israelites and compromises on God's opposition to idol worship. This pattern is repeated by his son, but this time the northern tribes rebel and the country is split into two:

Israel in the north and Judah in the south. The books of 1 & 2 Kings and 1 & 2 Chronicles work in parallel, narrating the stories of these kingdoms – how they swing between good and bad rulers, repeating the mistakes of the past and beginning to disintegrate. But when God can't lead his people directly, he speaks to them through the prophets. Figures like Elijah, Elisha and Amos in the north and, later, Isaiah and Jeremiah in the south speak up for God. They are voices for true worship and true justice, calling Israel back to the covenant with God and warning of a 'Day of the LORD' when his judgement would come.

Characters

Joshua: Joshua and Caleb (Numbers 13-14); God's commands (Joshua 1); the walls of Jericho (Joshua 6); Israel's choice (Joshua 24)
Gideon: Judges 6-7
Samson: Judges 13-16
Ruth: The book of Ruth
David: David's anointing (1 Samuel 16); David and Goliath (1 Samuel 17); David and Jonathan (1 Samuel 20); David dances (2 Samuel 6); God's promise (2 Samuel 7); David's sin (2 Samuel 11-12)
Solomon: Solomon's wisdom (1 Kings 3); the Queen of Sheba (1 Kings 10)
Elijah: 1 Kings 17-19; taken up to heaven (2 Kings 2)
Elisha: 2 Kings 2-8
Isaiah: his call (Isaiah 6)

Key Passages

Joshua 24:1-27 Joshua renews the covenant

After the death of Moses, Joshua led the people into Canaan (Palestine) – a fertile tract of land situated precariously between the trade routes of major powers. They defeated many of the local nations and claimed the territory. Here Joshua recounts God's faithful deeds and invites Israel to renew the covenant with God for themselves.

What would it mean for Israel to renew their covenant with God?

What does it mean for you to disavow all other idols and live in covenant with God (v. 24-25)?

Judges 2:6-23 The era of Judges
This passage sums up the whole era of Judges. God raised up heroic figures like Deborah, Gideon and Samson, but a deeper problem remained.
What was wrong with God's people at this time?

Why did God allow his people to suffer?

1 Samuel 8 Israel requests a king
Here's a mystery – the Israelites were faithless when they asked for a king, but without kings (Messiahs) there would be no David and no king Jesus. Is this another way in which God works with his people's limitations, even using their mistakes?
Why was it a bad move to ask for a king?

How do Samson's warnings ring true about the abuse of power in today's world?

1 Samuel 15:1-3, 7-31 God rejects Saul

The Amalekites were sworn enemies of Israel (see Exodus 17:8 & 14 and Judges 6:3). The only way forward for Israel at this time was to totally destroy certain enemies rather than making compromises with them. But instead of obeying God's instructions, Saul once again goes his own way. Perhaps more serious still, when challenged by Samuel he is reluctant to own up to the truth and repent. God requires more than this from the anointed leader of his people, so he rejects Saul for 'a man after his own heart' (13:14), who turns out in the next chapter to be young David.

What did Saul value most?

Are you wholehearted in obedience and quick to respond to correction?

🚌 2 Samuel 7:1-17 God's promise to David

Once David has united the tribes and established a new capital at Jerusalem, he seeks to build a Temple for the Lord. But God is no one's debtor. He refuses David's offer and instead promises him an everlasting royal line. It is Jesus, David's descendant, who finally and fully claimed the title of Christ (Messiah / anointed king).

Covenant	Mediator	Promise	Conditions
Between God & all creation	*Noah*	*Not to flood the earth again (Gen 9)*	*None*
Between God & Abraham's family	*Abraham*	*A nation of descendants and a land for them (Gen 12, 15, 17)*	*Circumcision*
Between God & Israel	*Moses*	*Blessings in the Promised Land (Exodus 19-24)*	*Obedience to God's law*
Between God & David;s line	*David*	*An everlasting royal line and world rule (2Samuel7)*	*None*

What is God's plan for his people, according to this passage?

Look at verses 8-9. How have you seen God's gracious blessing in your life up to this point?

2 Chronicles 7:1-6, 11-22 Solomon dedicates the Temple

Solomon built the first great temple in Jerusalem. Before this, the Israelites had approached God at various sanctuaries such as at Shiloh and Bethel. God wasn't confined to the Temple, but it was the centre of his presence on the earth, a special dwelling place for his glory, a piece of heaven on earth. In v13-22, God explains more about his conditions for living among his people.

Spend some time imagining this incredible scene. What does this passage tell you about the kind of God who dwelt in the Temple?

How can you bear this in mind when you approach God in worship?

1 Kings 11:41-12:24 The Kingdom splits

Bit by bit the politics of Israel self-destructed. Solomon was harsh, his son Rehoboam was unwise, and Jeroboam was rebellious. And so the kingdom splits in two: 10 northern tribes (sometimes called Israel, Ephraim or Samaria) and two southern tribes (often known as Judah or Jacob). By the end of this passage the two nations are at war and northern Israel turns to idols (12:25-33).

What lessons can be learned from this tragic split?

🚌 1 Kings 18:16-46 Elijah challenges Baal

Years down the line, the Northern Kingdom was still walking in idolatrous ways. Led by Ahab and his pagan wife Jezebel, worship of the fertility god Ball had become rife. God sends a 3-year drought and commissions the prophet Elijah to set up the ultimate confrontation between Yahweh (the LORD) and the so-called gods who would claim Israel's allegiance.

How is Yahweh (the LORD) different from Baal?

How do idols and other god-substitutes fail to deliver what they promise?

1 Kings 19:1-18 Elijah meets God

What strikes you from this famous passage?

Can you come to God now with Elijah's honesty and openness?

Old Testament Links

Psalm 23 The Lord is my Shepherd

The psalms are Hebrew songs, written with rhythmic or repeating phrases. They were first sung in the Temple, but by the time of Jesus had become a kind of national songbook. Many of the Psalms bear David's name; they were written by him or attributed to him.

Why not spend some time making the words of David's famous psalm your own?

Psalm 139 The presence of God

What signs of God's care can you see in this psalm?

How can you respond to these words in prayer now?

Proverbs 22:17-23:35 Wisdom for life

Proverbs, Ecclesiastes and Song of Songs are the great wisdom books linked with Solomon. Not all of these proverbs are intended as hard-and-fast rules; they are meant to be read together as wise insights and guide-lines for good living.

Which proverb stands out for you? Why not commit it to memory?

Isaiah 11:1-9 A Messiah prophesied

After a succession of disappointing kings, a new dream arose of a king truly blessed by God. Here Isaiah, speaking in the Southern capital Jerusalem, foretells a great Messiah. Somehow, through this king, God will set the whole world to rights and bring his amazing future - the age to come.
What is so wonderful about this Messiah?

NEW TESTAMENT LINKS

Acts 2:22-36 Jesus made both Lord and Christ

When Peter stood up before the people of Jerusalem on the day of Pentecost, just weeks after Jesus had been raised from the dead, he was able to confirm that Jesus is God's true Messiah (v. 36). Somehow God's promises to David were too great for David himself to fulfil. The first disciples soon realized that Jesus was the 'Lord' David was speaking about (v. 34, see Matthew 22:41-46); he was the culmination of the hopes of the ages and had now triumphed over the greatest enemy of God's people: death itself.
What does it mean for you to live with Jesus as Lord and King?

The Promised Land: Group Discussion

Study Passage: 2 Samuel 7:1-17

What strikes you from this passage?

What kind of God comes through in Nathan's prophecy?

How is Jesus prefigured in these words?

How have you seen God's grace and promises at work in your own life?

Questions for Reflection

How has God been speaking to you about himself and the Big Story?

What has challenged or inspired you?

The third episode of the Big Story crystallizes the contest between the one true God and all other idols; it also illustrates God's desire for us to live wisely and well before him.
How can you see these themes playing out in your life?

The Kings of Israel and Judah

	KINGS OF	UNITED ISRAEL	
C11th BC		**Saul**	*Samuel*
		David	*Nathan*
C10th BC		**Solomon**	
	KINGS OF JUDAH	**KINGS OF ISRAEL**	
	(see especially I & II Chronicles)	(see especially I & II Kings)	
	Rehoboam	**Jeroboam**	
	Abijah		
	Asa		
		Nadab	
C9th		Baasha	
		Elah	
		Zimri	
		Omri & Tibni	*Elijah*
		Ahab (&Jezebel)	
	Jehosophat		
		Ahaziah	
		Joram	*Elisha*
	Jehoram		
	Ahaziah		
		Jehu	
	Queen Athaliah		
	Joash		
C8th		Jehoahaz	
		Jehoash	
	Amaziah		
		Jeroboam II	*Hosea* *cont. . .*

The Kings of Israel and Judah

.. cont	**KINGS OF JUDAH**		**KINGS OF ISRAEL**
	Uzziah (Azariah)	*Isaiah*	
			Zechariah
			Shallum
			Menahem
			Pekahiah
			Pekah
	Jotham	*Micah*	
	Ahaz		
			Hoshea
			Fall of Israel 722 BC
C7th	**Hezekiah**		
	Manasseh		
	Amon		
	Josiah	*Zephaniah*	
		Jeremiah	
	Jehoahaz		
	Jehoiakim	*Habakkuk*	
	(Taken to Babylon 597)		
C6th	Jehoiachin		
	Zedekiah		
	Fall of Jerusalem 586 BC		

Prophets are shown in italics. Kings whose reigns were considered good by the biblical authors include David, Asa (2 Chr 14-16), Jehosophat (2 Chr 17-20), Hezekiah (2 Chr 29-32) and Josiah (2 Chr 34-35).

Episode 4
Exile and Return
EZRA - MALACHI

Overview

The Old Testament doesn't come to a climax with a mighty and united kingdom of Israel; it ends in failure. The prophets warn of God's judgement, but the only thing that unites the two kingdoms is their idolatry and political insecurity. First the northern kingdom, Israel, is invaded by the mighty Assyria. In 722BC the capital, Samaria, is captured and many Israelites are deported and dispersed. Still, in the South, other prophets warn Judah's leaders to turn to the LORD and his ways. A few kings (like Hezekiah and Josiah) bring reforms, but eventually Judah too is invaded, this time by Assyria's successor - the Babylonian Empire. Judah's king is captured in 597BC, and then in 586BC Jerusalem is ransacked and burned, and many Jews are exiled in Babylon.

Who can capture the horror of this experience? The land God promised is invaded and lost, the Temple in which his presence dwelt is destroyed, Jerusalem - the city of God - smolders in ruins, and all because God's people have failed in their calling to live for him. Three great prophets and their followers live around this time: Isaiah sees it coming (Isaiah ch 1-39); Ezekiel is taken to Babylon with the ruling elite; and Jeremiah has to suffer the horrific invasion at first hand.

The exile is a desperate time for the people of God, but it is also a time to plumb the depths of God's mercy. Somehow, far from their homeland, God is still with them, keeping them safe. This is Daniel's story, as a servant of God in the court of the Babylonian king. Even in this dark place there is a light. The earlier prophets had spoken of a great restoration, and now in exile other prophets pick up this theme. The later chapters of Isaiah, Ezekiel and Jeremiah speak a word of hope to the captives. They will return. God has not given up on his people or his plan to bless the world through them.

And so it is that the Babylonians are conquered by the Persians who grant the Jews the right to return to their homeland. After over half a century of exile, and against all the odds, the captives begin to return and commence the slow process of rebuilding. Ezra and Haggai encourage the building of a second Temple and Nehemiah supervises the repair of Jerusalem's walls. But the faith of Israel also needs rebuilding, so many prophecies at this time (for example, Malachi and the last chapters of Isaiah) speak of the need for renewal in Israel's religion.

The land God promised is lost, the Temple is destroyed, Jerusalem smolders in ruins

As the Old Testament period draws to a close, the great restoration of God's people still hasn't happened - Israel's position is unstable and her tribes are still scattered. Where is the awesome day of the LORD and the glorious age to come? Where is the mighty Messiah? Where is the great victory promised to God's people?

Characters

Jeremiah: his call (Jeremiah 1); Jeremiah rejected (Jeremiah 36-38)
Daniel: taken to Babylon (Daniel 1); the lion's den (Daniel 6)
Ezra: Ezra reads the law (Nehemiah 8)
Nehemiah: his prayer and request (Nehemiah 1-2)
Esther: Esther helps the Jews (Esther 4)

Key Passages

Amos 5 Judgement on Israel

When the kings of Israel failed to rule justly, the prophets spoke up. Increasingly their words were gathered by their followers in books like this one. Here Amos, a shepherd from the southern kingdom, came north to speak the unspeakable. If Israel would not live as God's people, then one day he would no longer be their God.

How are the people of God called to live, according to this passage?

How might this translate practically today?

🚍 2 Kings 17:1-23 Northern Israel invaded and deported

Despite some periods of expansion and prosperity, the northern kingdom was invaded by Assyria. Throughout the Old Testament changes in politics are narrated with hindsight from a God's-eye-view: this isn't just another victory by a great military empire, it is a judgement from God.

What are the real reasons for Israel's destruction?

🚍 2 Chronicles 36:11-23 Judah exiled

Eventually, the unthinkable happened to Judah, too, but this time they were taken captive by the Babylonians. The cruelty of the Babylonians is total, but in a strange way even the land itself is pleased to see God's unfaithful people go (verse 21).

What does God show about his character through these events?

Lamentations 1:1-11, 3:19-33 The deserted city

This poetic lament captures the experience of exile in all its horror. Chapter one pictures Jerusalem as a disgraced woman, while in chapter three the shame of the author is a symbol for the feelings of a nation. And yet even here there is somehow hope…

What experiences of failure, abandonment or shame have you known?

Can you pray the words of 3:19-33 over the darkest times of your life?

Daniel 3:1, 8-30 The fiery furnace

Though some poorer Israelites remained in Judea, many Jews were taken to serve the Babylonian Empire. Daniel and the three men mentioned here - Shadrach, Meshach and Abednego – adopted Babylonian names (see 1:7) and served the king, but they drew the line at idolatry. As they took their stand in a hostile place, somehow God was with them.

What strikes you from this story?

Is there a hostile environment or workplace where you need God's help or protection?

Daniel 7:1-18 One like a Son of Man

In Daniel's enigmatic dream God confers a kingdom on his chosen people, despite the raging of world powers and the sufferings of the saints. In the centuries after the exile, during times of oppression by Persians, Greeks and Romans, the Jewish people drew strength from the words of this chapter. The figure 'like a son of man' stands for the whole people of God who survive great persecution. But Jesus claimed these words for himself (see Mark 14:61-2) – he is the one who deserves all honour and worship; he is the one who will win the victory for God's people.

Let this scene unfold before your mind. How does this passage give you courage and hope?

Jeremiah 31:21-34 A new covenant

Covenant	Mediator	Promise	Conditions
Between God & all creation	*Noah*	*Not to flood the earth again (Gen 9)*	*None*
Between God & Abraham's family	*Abraham*	*A nation of descendants and a land for them (Gen 12, 15, 17)*	*Circumcision*
Between God & Israel	*Moses*	*Blessings in the Promised Land (Exodus 19-24)*	*Obedience to God's law*
Between God & David;s line	*David*	*An everlasting royal line and world rule (2Samuel7)*	*None*
A new convenant . .	*?*	*Forgiveness of sins and a new heart (Jeremiah 31)*	

God's covenants with Israel through Abraham and Moses seemed to have ended in failure. But his promise here is earth-shattering – a new cove-

nant. Israel and Judah will be united once more, rescued from exile, and (most importantly) God will give them the ability to at last fulfil his commands.

What will be the marks of the new covenant?

Ezra 1:1-4, 3:8-13 Return to Jerusalem

Solomon's Temple had been a highpoint of Israel's history, but this second Temple is not quite the same. Israel has returned from exile, but the dramatic promises of a wonderful new covenant have yet to come true. In a way, Israel is still in exile, waiting for the LORD to save his people once and for all.

In what ways has God shown that 'his love to Israel endures forever' (v. 11)?

Verse 13 mixes joy and tears. Has there been a mix of joy and tears in your walk with God?

Nehemiah 1 Rebuilding the walls

As the exile drew to a close and the Babylonian Empire fell to the Persians, some Jews still remained in exile, like Nehemiah in Susa (one of Persia's royal cities). Jerusalem's broken walls mean that God's people are still weak and defenceless, despite having returned to the land.

What can you learn from the way Nehemiah prayed?

OLD TESTAMENT LINKS

Job 19 I know that my redeemer lives

Like the exile, the tale of Job (the man who loses everything) raises the question of God's justice, especially as Job had done nothing wrong (see Job 1). Here Job defends himself against the charge that suffering is always deserved. His poetic speeches give us a glimpse into a heart that trusts God whatever comes. Despite the darkness of his trials, Job believes that God will act justly in the end and will clear the names of his faithful servants.

What strikes you from this profound chapter?

Isaiah 40 Comfort, comfort my people

When the time of exile was completed, the message of judgement was replaced by a message of comfort. These words, addressed to the exiles in Babylon, must have fallen like a mighty waterfall of grace over God's people.

Imagine what it must have been like to hear this prophecy. What brings you comfort?

Isaiah 42:1-9 A light to the gentiles

The story was not over for Israel. God's purpose for them remained – Israel was still God's servant (see 41:8-10). God's plan had always been that his people would be a blessing to the world. Here he calls them 'a light to the Gentiles' – somehow Israel would be used to bring the whole world back to God. But how?

What inspires you about this description of the people of God?

Jesus said, 'you are the light of the world...let your light shine before others, that they may see your good deeds and glorify your Father in heaven' (Matthew 5:14, 16). How can you be a light to those around you?

Malachi 2:17-3:5, 4:1-6 The day of the LORD

After the return from exile, prophets like Malachi and Haggai still called God's people to put him first. The fact that God would come to his people was both a promise and a threat: there was more to come, but God

wouldn't put up with imperfect standards forever.
What would be the signs of the day of the LORD?

NEW TESTAMENT LINKS

Luke 4:14-21 Good news for the poor

The prophecy Jesus reads from was given by Isaiah about Israel one day returning from exile and being wonderfully saved by God (Is 61). 500 years after the return from exile, Jesus claims that these distant dreams are at last coming true. God would do something through Jesus to finally take Israel's shame away and enable God's people to be all they were called to be.
How did Jesus' ministry fulfil these words?

What signs of the kingdom can you pray for now?

Exile & Return: Group Discussion

Study Passage: Jeremiah 31:15-34

What strikes you from this passage?

Why is the new covenant so important?

Have you experienced what it's like to be far from God or disciplined by him?

What has been your experience of the new covenant Jeremiah prophesied?

Questions for Reflection

How has God been speaking to you about himself and the Big Story?

What has challenged or inspired you?

The fourth episode of the Big Story contains suffering, tears and the absence of God; we also see God's passion for faithful living and just societies.
How can you see these themes playing out in your life?

Episode 5
The Kingdom of God

The Gospels: Part I (Matthew 1-25; Mark 1-13; Luke 1-21; John 1-17)

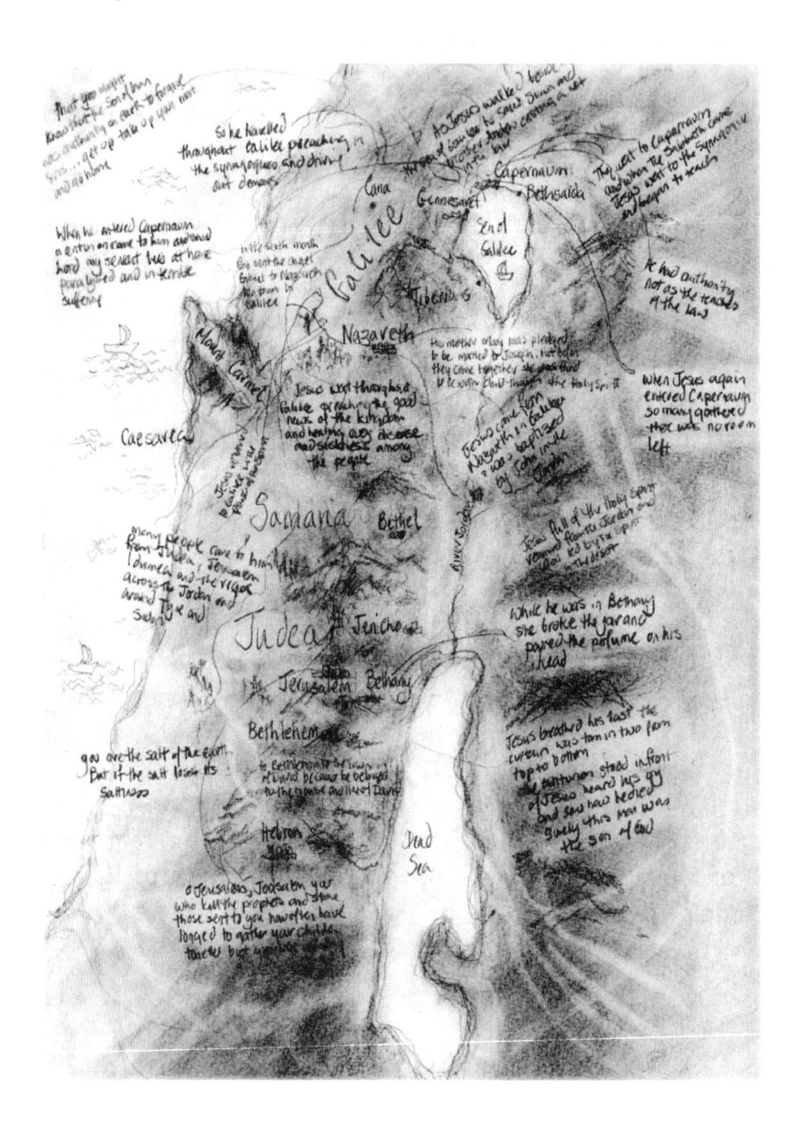

Overview

How can God set all things back to rights? How can he complete the story? Only by joining it. The life of Jesus is about God getting his hands dirty, walking among us, showing how life should be lived and what love looks like. It's about God being willing to join humanity to himself no matter what the cost. To do this, God had to become one of us. This is the incarnation - God made flesh - and it begins with Mary's miraculous pregnancy and the birth of Jesus into a normal Israelite family.

Everything we get wrong, Jesus got right

The time of Jesus (centuries after the last Old Testament books) finds the Jewish people still in Palestine, but under Roman occupation. After returning from exile, God's people have been ruled by Persian and Greek powers, with only a brief taste of independence. Many still long for freedom and for God's Messiah to bring the kingdom.

This is the world Jesus is born into, a world marked by oppression and longing, a world fractured by sin. And in this broken world Jesus walks the path of obedience. Everything sinful humans get wrong, Jesus gets right.

Following his baptism, Jesus brings the announcement of the age - the kingdom of God has drawn near. This is his 'good news' (or gospel). God is coming to rule, coming to save his people at last and to bring things on earth to be 'as it is in heaven'. John the Baptist had heralded the kingdom, but Jesus brings it with him. He heals the sick, casts out demons, forgives sins, and invites every kind of person to make a new start with God. It's the news God's people had been waiting for. But it comes strangely. It's a time for feasting, but not just with respectable people; it's a time for forgiveness, but not from the Temple as usual; it's Israel's dream, but not as she expected it - everything is upside down.

And so Jesus wins enemies as well as friends. His plan for Israel isn't the mighty revolution many dreamed of. Instead of conquering the world, Israel will be a light to the world by living out God's love. So Jesus calls 12 disciples, and others, to be a new kind of Israel. He schools them in the ways of the kingdom, and he sends them out to preach the good news and heal in his name. Jesus' ministry begins like this, with his disciples around Galilee. It comes to a highpoint when Peter confesses that Jesus is the Messiah, followed by a glimpse of Jesus' glory on a mountain. From this point, Jesus starts out on the long road to Jerusalem to face his destiny.

Characters

Mary: her faith and her song (Luke 1)
John the Baptist: his birth (Luke 3); his message (Matthew 4)
Jesus
The disciples: called (Luke 5-6); sent out (Luke 9-10)

Key Passages

John 1:1-14 The Word became flesh

Here are two sides of one mystery: firstly, God is not alone in himself – the Word was with him and involved in creation (v. 1-3); secondly, humanity is not isolated from God – the Word (God's own thought or his self-expression) has become flesh in Jesus Christ (v. 14). Now there will always been a connection between God and humanity, and the way is open for us to come to him.

What verses here give you an insight into who Jesus is?

Why not turn them into prayer and praise?

Luke 3:1-20 John the Baptist

The good news of the kingdom has a double-effect: on the one hand, the Lord returns to Israel (v. 4) bringing forgiveness and his Spirit; on the other hand, there is the warning of judgement and the need for repentance. To repent means to change your mind and your life (see v. 10-14).
What stands out to you from John's words?

Where is God calling you to bring your life under his government?

Matthew 3:13-4:11 Baptism and temptation

Jesus walked the human path in every way, even being baptised alongside sinful people. But he always obeyed his Father, which is why God's Spirit could rest so fully on him. The devil seeks to test this perfect relationship, but unlike Adam in the garden and Israel in the wilderness, Jesus remains faithful. He is God's true Son and the perfect Israelite.
What does the devil use to try to throw Jesus off course?

How does Jesus overcome temptation?

Mark 1:14-20 Announcing the Kingdom

The 'good news' Jesus declares is that God is returning to Israel to save them from the mess they were in and to bring their history to a climax. This is the kingdom of God, where God takes his rightful place as King and sets the world to rights, starting right in the midst of his people. After many centuries of waiting, now the time had come (v. 15).

In what ways did Jesus set things right?

How do you feel about Jesus calling you to be a messenger of his kingdom?

Luke 5:17-26 Who is this?

God's people had been used to going to the Temple for forgiveness, making a sacrifice and approaching God through a priest. Jesus cuts through the whole system – he brings the presence and power of God directly to people at their point of need. This was hard for people to grasp, which is why Jesus backs up his claim with an incredible healing.

What kinds of authority does Jesus show in this passage?

What different reactions to Jesus are evident in this account?

Matthew 5:1-12 Blessed are the poor in spirit
We all have ideas about who is truly blessed: the rich, the satisfied, the comfortable, the powerful. In Jesus' day, many Jews thought God's kingdom would bless Israel with a powerful military triumph over their oppressors. Jesus turns all this on its head. He offered God's blessing to a downtrodden people, but on different terms. God is looking to bless a much less likely bunch than we might think, and he seeks to build a radically different kind of people.
Who does our society believe are the blessed ones?

What is different about what Jesus is saying?

Which of these blessings encourages you? Which challenges you?

Matthew 6 The sermon on the mount
Matthew 5-7 is a collection of Jesus' teaching on how life works in the kingdom of God. Here Jesus sets out the real way for Israel to please God and the lifestyle he has been looking for since the very beginning.
What strikes you from this chapter?

Luke 10:1-24 Sending the disciples

Though Jesus alone could bring the kingdom, he called disciples (earlier the 12 and here 72) to preach the message and perform miracles as signs of God's rule. As they went, something spread with urgency and wonder through Israel, and the presence of Jesus went with them (v. 16-17). Not all the conditions are the same for us today, but the basic task still remains.

What can you learn from Jesus' instructions about being a messenger for him?

Where could God be sending you as an ambassador for him?

Mark 8:27-9:1 Who do you say I am?

People weren't expecting a Messiah anything like this, and so Jesus often kept his calling secret. But the things he did, and his words at times like this, show that he was indeed the Messiah – Israel's true King sent from God himself. There would come a public vindication, too (9:1). Powerful evidence of the kingdom was on its way – glimpsed in the transfiguration (following this passage), manifest in Jesus' resurrection, and demonstrated as the warnings and promises of Jesus' ministry came true in the lifetimes of his disciples.

'But what about you? Who do you say I am?' What would you reply?

Matthew 17:1-13 The transfiguration

This unforgettable happening is a preview of the glory Jesus would have at his resurrection and ascension to the Father's glory. Once again God sets the record straight about the identity of his Son –encouraging both him and his disciples.

Put yourself in the disciple's shoes. What was their experience of Jesus in this incident?

Are you aware of the surpassing glory of who Jesus is? How could you 'listen to him' more (v. 5)?

Luke 15:1-2, 11-32 The prodigal son and the welcoming Father

The exile had been a scattering for Israel, but now Jesus gathers. He offers a new start for everyone that doesn't depend on following the strict Jewish purity rules that had been developed. There was no more powerful sign of this grace-filled welcome, in that culture, than eating with those labeled 'sinners' (v. 2). Jesus celebrates the feast of God's kingdom, but the guest list includes anyone who's willing to come (see 14:15-24). Here Jesus appeals to his opponents to recognise what God is doing through his work.

What kind of God comes across in this parable?

Do you feel you have a place in God's family? Are you in touch with heaven's joy over your rescue (v. 7)?

Old Testament Links

Ezekiel 34:1-16, 20-24 The shepherd will come

The shepherds of Israel were her leaders. At the time of the exile, when Ezekiel spoke, God promised that one day he would come to shepherd his people himself. Centuries later, Jesus claimed, 'I am the good shepherd' (John 10:11).

How does Jesus fulfil Ezekiel's words?

New Testament Links

2 Corinthians 8:1-9 The generosity of God

The incarnation (God made flesh) is more than just a belief for Paul. It inspires him to live differently, following the pattern of his Saviour (see verse 9). The poverty Christ chose was both to live with our weaknesses and to die for our sins. Because of this we can be truly rich.
How would you describe the generosity of God?

What would it mean for you to live with open-handed generosity, as Jesus did?

Hebrews 4:14-5:10 One who sympathizes

Old Testament high priests were just like the other Israelites – though they could sympathize with others, their sacrifices were tainted by sin. Jesus is a new kind of high priest – a perfect one (which is what the writer means by 'a priest in the order of Melchizedek'). He feels for us in every situation, yet he was fully obedient to God and so he can save us. There's no part of human life that Jesus didn't share, so there is nothing that can't somehow be set right by him.
According to this passage, what did Jesus go through for us?

The Kingdom of God: Group Discussion

Study Passage: Matthew 16:13-28

What strikes you from this passage?

How does Jesus fulfil Israel's hopes in this passage? How does he challenge them?

What is the cost of the kingdom, for Jesus and his followers?

What does this mean for us today?

Questions for Reflection

How has God been speaking to you about himself and the Big Story?

What has challenged or inspired you?

In the fifth episode of the Big Story we see the kingdom's power to rescue and restore; but we also see the clash between the kingdom's values and those of the surrounding culture.
How can you see these themes playing out in your life?

Episode 6

The Cross of Christ

The Gospels: Part II (Matthew 26-27; Mark 14-15; Luke 22-23; John 18-19)

Overview

Now the story comes to its climax. God has entered our story in Jesus of Nazareth, reaching out to Israel at their lowest point. But still they didn't respond. Many turn away, and some are prepared to kill him. And so, having travelled from heaven to earth, there is one more journey the Son of God must make, and make alone. Somehow the evil which infects the world must be brought into the open and met head-on, it must do its worst in God's own self and so finally be defeated. This is the story of the cross.

In the final chapters of each gospel, Jesus arrives with his band of followers in Jerusalem. He marches into the city and confronts its leaders and the corrupt Temple system. While the authorities conspire against him, Jesus and his followers celebrate the freedom feast of God's people - the Passover - only this time the price of freedom will be the body and blood of Jesus himself. After this point, everyone seems to turn against Jesus. He is tried, beaten, ridiculed, flogged and condemned to death.

In the darkness of tragedy, God is strangely at work

In human terms, the cross is an event of torture and shame that publicly stamps Jesus' career with failure. Israel's Messiah was supposed to triumph mightily, not die as a criminal. And yet somehow, in the darkness of the tragedy, God is strangely at work. Jesus had pointed forward to his death, obedience had led him to it, the scriptures had prophesied it.

So why does Jesus have to die? There is simply no other way. Sin must be dealt with, evil has to be destroyed. How can humans live forever with a perfect God unless their sins are paid for in full? But who can pay this debt except someone whose life isn't tainted by sin? And so Jesus, God's own Son, offers himself as the payment - the ransom to set us free. On the cross all the ugly destructiveness of sin takes its toll on the only innocent man who ever lived. Jesus endures God's judgement on sinful humanity; he suffers the fate we all deserve; he dies in our place. And as he dies, the most spectacular victory in all history is won. Sin and death, the ultimate enemies of God's people, exhaust themselves in the broken body of the Messiah. Because of this, sin and death have no final power over Jesus Christ, or anyone who belongs to him, or his plans for creation. Such is the power of the cross.

The writers of the New Testament never forget the cross of Christ. It shows things as they really are - the depth of human rebellion (even by God's own people), but also the strength of God's love. The cross reminds us what love looks like in a broken world. And Jesus warned his disciples that they, too, must walk the way of the cross, letting go of their old life and trusting God whatever comes.

Key Passages

Matthew 26:17-30 The Last Supper

Covenant	Mediator	Promise	Conditions
Between God & all creation	*Noah*	*Not to flood the earth again (Gen 9)*	*None*
Between God & Abraham's family	*Abraham*	*A nation of descendants and a land for them (Gen 12, 15, 17)*	*Circumcision*
Between God & Israel	*Moses*	*Blessings in the Promised Land (Exodus 19-24)*	*Obedience to God's law*
Between God & David;s line	*David*	*An everlasting royal line and world rule (2Samuel7)*	*None*
Between God & many people	*Jesus*	*Forgiveness of sins and a new heart (Jeremiah 31; Matthew 26)*	*Repentance and faith in Jesus*

This is the last and greatest covenant between God and his people, and the true fulfilment of all God's promises to Abraham. The new covenant would enable Jesus' disciples and many others to be with him when the

kingdom comes (v. 29), even though none of us deserve it. What makes this covenant so strong? Jesus underwrites it with his own blood (the covenant sacrifice). Not only that, he has already completed our side of the bargain by offering up a life of perfect obedience to God in our place.
According to this passage, what makes sharing bread and wine so special?

John 13:1-17 The full extent of his love
Here is another twist in the tale of God. Jesus, despite all his power and glory, shows the full extent of his love by washing the mucky feet of his followers. This is a new picture of who God is, and the lengths he is prepared to go to. Secure in who he was (v. 3), Jesus was free to serve – and we should be the same.
What do you imagine it would feel like to have Jesus wash your feet?

What does it mean for us to 'wash one another's feet'?

Mark 14:32-42 Gethsemane
Here we glimpse Jesus' relationship with 'Abba' (the actual Aramaic word for Father that Jesus used). At this point Jesus fully realised the

task before him, and yet he was willing to go on. The cup is a symbol for God's judgement that he didn't deserve, but God's people did.
What do you notice about Jesus' relationship with God?

Mark 14:53-65, 15:1-15 Trial and torture
This is the big confrontation – Jesus versus the so-called rulers of the God's people (the Sanhedrin) and the world (the Romans). Instead of being recognised and exonerated, Jesus is condemned. But by rejecting God's innocent Son, the human powers actually condemn themselves.
What do you see in Jesus through these events?

John 19:16-30 It is finished
John wants us to know that throughout these cruel and chaotic events, a larger hand is at work. God's purpose, set out in scripture, is being fulfilled. And so, when he dies, Jesus can cry, 'it is finished' – at last he has accomplished the saving plan of God.
What is your reaction to the death of Jesus?

OLD TESTAMENT LINKS

Isaiah 52:13-53:12 The suffering servant

This chapter spoke to God's crushed people at the time of exile in Babylon. Isaiah dreamed that one day the sufferings of God's people would have a purpose. But for many centuries none of God's people lived up to this description. After witnessing the cross, the early Christians soon realised that only one person could.

How does Jesus fit this prophecy?

What do these verses reveal about the power of the cross?

NEW TESTAMENT LINKS

Romans 3:21-26 Justified freely by his grace

Throughout history a dilemma has remained: everyone has sinned and God, being just, can't allow sin to remain unpunished forever. How can God save his people without simply excusing their sin? This is why Jesus handed himself over to suffer in our place. Thanks to him, despite our sins, we can be justified - included in God's family by grace.

Why not spend some time dwelling on the forgiveness brought by the cross?

Romans 6:1-14 A new life

Does forgiveness give us a license to sin? NO, cries Paul. Forgiveness only comes by being united with Jesus Christ. If we're united with Jesus, then somehow we died on that cross, too. Our old life and our old securities were left behind when we were baptised. Now we have a new purpose – to live for God – and this should be our focus.

When were you baptised? What does it mean to you?

What has died in you since you 'died with Christ' (v. 8)?

Are there any ways in which sin is still 'your master' (v. 14)?

2 Corinthians 4:7-18 Power and weakness

The Christians in Corinth were disappointed with Paul. Instead of impressive words and a successful life, he faced trial upon trial. But Paul saw something deeper in his life – the death of Christ and his resurrection life both at work at the same time. The Christian life is always like this: a mix of pain on the one hand and power on the other.

What gave Paul hope in his struggles?

2 Corinthians 5:11-6:2 New creation in Christ

Paul pleads with the Corinthians to realise what the death of Jesus means. It means we can no longer live by human appearances or by selfish desires that ruin our relationships. The cross brings us into a new world of forgiveness, won by Christ, where every believer is an act of new creation begun by God (v. 17).

What strikes you from Paul's explanation of the cross?

Look carefully at the passage. What does it mean to be a new creation (v. 17)?

Hebrews 2:10-15 Victory over Satan

For Jesus to be able to save us, he had to suffer alongside the rest of the human race, even to the point of death. By coming so close to us he won the right to wrap up our lives in his. Because of this, everyone in Jesus' family can come through death, just like he did. Now we don't have to fear death, or the devil – his power has been broken and he is marked out for destruction.

In what ways are people slaves to the fear of death today?

What can be different now Satan's power is broken?

Hebrews 10:11-25 Jesus our priest

In the Old Testament era, priests were needed to continually offer sacrifices for sin (v. 11). Like a priest, Jesus offered a perfect sacrifice – his innocent life. This is the sacrifice that underpins God's new covenant with his people (Hebrews 8:7-13). Now Jesus has made it possible to draw near to God and be forgiven without any animal sacrifices, once and for all.

What encouragement do you get from this passage?

Why not draw near to God now in assurance that you can be cleansed 'from a guilty conscience' (v. 22)?

1 Peter 2:18-25 Example and exchange

When we suffer, we don't have to give our life in exchange for the sins of the world as Jesus did (v. 24). But we are called to follow Jesus' example.

Is there any unjust suffering you have had to cope with?

What does it mean for you to 'follow in his steps' (v. 21)?

Revelation 5 The Lamb is worthy

In John's vision, he sees a scroll that can unlock the world's destiny, but no one can open the scroll and bring that destiny to pass. Only Jesus can solve this problem. He is Israel's true king (the lion – v. 5) but also a perfect sacrifice (the lamb - v. 6) who died for others. At last, God's purpose for the universe can go forward and people from round the world can take their special place with him (v. 9-10).

Let John's image affect your imagination. Can you sense the wonder of what Jesus has done?

What will you say to Jesus, knowing that he is enthroned now in heaven?

The Cross of Christ: Group Discussion

Study Passage: 2 Corinthians 5:11-6:2

What strikes you from this passage?

According to Paul, what effects does the death of Christ have?

What practical difference does the cross of Christ make to Paul's life and (he hopes) to the Corinthians?

What does it mean for you to live as a 'new creation' (v. 17)?

Questions for Reflection

How has God been speaking to you about himself and the Big Story?

What has challenged or inspired you?

The sixth episode of the Big Story features God's victory over darkness, his provision of forgiveness, and the path of sacrificial love that sets others free.
How can you see these themes playing out in your life?

Episode 7
Resurrection and the Church

The Gospels: Part III (Matthew 28; Mark 16; Luke 24; John 20-21), ACTS-REVELATION 3

Overview

Our story hit its deepest point with the cross of Christ, and now it reaches its most incredible. The laws of nature are broken, the true identity of Jesus is breathtakingly revealed, and somehow the glorious goal of all history makes an advance appearance.

The resurrection appearances are impossible to prove, but even harder to dismiss

The resurrection of Jesus isn't an escape from death; it isn't promotion to an angelic state; but it isn't a return to normal life either. What happens on Easter Sunday is this: Jesus rises from death to a new life. His risen life is real human life, but free from the influence of sin and death. It's the eternal life we were destined for. But it is possible to share it. God's Son has united himself to humanity by walking with us and dying for us. So now we can follow his path - through death into that same kind of glorious risen life.

The resurrection appearances at the end of the gospels are full of mystery and miracle: impossible to prove, but even harder to dismiss. A few weeks of meetings with Jesus transform the disciples, whose dreams had been shattered by the shameful death of their leader. When Jesus ascends to be with the Father, he leaves his followers with an unshakeable conviction that he is now beginning to take charge of the world, driving out his defeated enemies - sin and Satan - and bringing new creation in their place.

But what will be the power behind this new creation? God gives his answer on the day of Pentecost, by pouring out his Spirit on the church (Acts 2). Luke picks up this story in Acts and explains the spread of Christianity. The message of repentance and faith in Jesus goes out first to Jews (Acts 3-9), but gradually the disciples realise that God is at last calling all people to himself - Jew and Gentile alike (Acts 15). The chief instrument in this process is Paul. Commissioned by Jesus in a belated resurrection appearance, Paul goes on several missionary journeys, starting and encouraging Gentile churches across the Mediterranean (Acts 16-20) before eventually facing trial (Acts 21-28).

These new communities of believers are the fledgling Christian church, and most of the New Testament is made up of letters written to them or their leaders by apostles like Paul, James, Peter and John. The churches are places of transformation, where Jew and Gentile together live the lifestyle of the kingdom. They are marked out by prayer and miracles, love, joy and renewed lives. But they are also far from perfect, struggling with conflict and confusion, and facing opposition from others. They live, as we do now, in between the ages – the old order is dying, the new age is beginning.

Characters

Peter: his call (Luke 5:1-11); walking on water (Matthew 14:22-26); faith (Mark 8:27-10); denial (Mark 14:66-72) and restoration (John 21:15-23); preaching at Pentecost (Acts 2); his dream (Acts 10)
Paul: his conversion (Acts 9); his first missionary journey (Acts 13-14); his second journey (Acts 16-18); his third journey (Acts 20-21); his trials (Acts 22-28)
Barnabas and Luke

Key Passages

Matthew 28:1-20 Resurrection and the great commission

Easter Sunday (the first day of the Jewish week) is the scene of a breathtaking new beginning. Many Jews expected the resurrection of the dead, but not like this – one man ahead of all the rest. Each gospel names the eyewitnesses whose reports they're using. The accounts the gospel writers compiled are raw, detailed and occasionally slightly confusing (perhaps this is unsurprising given the nature of the events!). But none of the witnesses is in any doubt that they saw the empty tomb and met the risen Jesus in person. This passage contains their testimony to us,

and also a commission from Jesus – to make followers for him from every nation. There's an early reference to the Trinity in verse 19.
What eyewitness details do you notice in Matthew's account?

What challenges or encourages you from Jesus' great commission (v. 18-20)?

Acts 1:1-11 The ascension

The risen Jesus sends his disciples out to the immediate area (Jerusalem); and to the whole of Israel (not just Judea but Samaria too – where the remnants of Israel's old northern kingdom remained); and also to the ends of the earth to bring the Gentiles to God at last.
How do you feel about being a witness for Christ?

What encouragement does he give to all his witnesses?

Acts 2:1-24, 36-47 Pentecost and the early church

The Holy Spirit is God himself living in his people. This is what Israel had always lacked, relying instead on prophets and priests to know

God, and struggling to keep his laws. Now the risen Lord Jesus was responsible for the Spirit being poured out more abundantly than ever before. This, and the resurrection, proved that Jesus was God's Messiah.
What does the Holy Spirit reveal about himself in this passage?

What strikes you about the life of the church in verses 42-47?

Acts 9:1-19 Paul's conversion

The early Christian movement (called 'the Way' v. 2) was opposed by many Jews like Saul, who wanted Israel to stick rigidly to Old Testament law. Like many, Saul believed that a crucified criminal couldn't be God's Messiah. To find out that Jesus was in fact reigning with God was the shock of Saul's life and led to a total rethink of his priorities.
What does this passage show about how God calls people to serve him?

Are you ready, like Saul and Ananias, to follow God's lead in reaching out to others?

🚌 Acts 10:9-48 Cornelius - the first Gentile believer

Here is a great turning point in the history of God's people. Nearly 2,000 years after God called Abraham and his family, membership in the family of God is now open to all, regardless of circumcision, food laws, or ritual purity. But this was incredibly hard for Jewish believers to grasp as it meant rethinking many cherished traditions.

What are the signs of God's work in Cornelius' life throughout this passage?

How might God be calling you to rethink cherished practices and to reach out beyond boundaries?

Acts 17:16-34 The message in Athens

Paul took the gospel about Jesus out into the cities of the Mediterranean. He challenged people to turn from the worship of many gods, and an immoral lifestyle, to the one true God revealed in Israel's story and known through Jesus.

How does Paul encourage the Athenians in his speech (v. 24-31)?

How does he challenge them?

Old Testament Links

Ezekiel 37:1-14 Resurrection for a lifeless people

Ezekiel's vision during the exile spoke to a people whose faith lay in ruins. First of all it promised a return from Babylon. Secondly, God's Spirit would live in his people so they could follow his commands (v. 14; see 36:26 - 'I will give you a new heart and put a new spirit in you; I will remove from you your heart of stone and give you a heart of flesh'). Finally, passages like this began to make the Jews hope for something they'd never dared to believe before – that one day the Lord would actually raise his people to new life after death.

What does the promise of resurrection mean to you?

How does this passage speak to times of hopelessness in your life or in the lives of those around you?

New Testament Links

John 14:15-31 Jesus promises the Spirit

Jesus revealed that God is Father, Son and Holy Spirit ('the Spirit of truth' v. 17). In one way, God's Spirit is present everywhere in this world, giving life to all things. But in another way, the Spirit must come and live inside each of us (v. 17).

According to Jesus, what will the Spirit do?

In what ways would you like to know more of God's Spirit in your life? Can you ask for this now (and also ask others to pray with you for it)?

1 Corinthians 15:12-28 Jesus raised and reigning

Some of the Corinthian church had taken to doubting that the dead will be raised, but Paul defends it robustly (v. 12-19). He looks back with dismay at the influence of Adam – one man's sin ruined God's good plans (v. 22). But now he also looks back with joy at the influence of Christ – one man's obedience will save many people. Christ is the 'firstfruits'; the first part of the harvest guaranteeing that one day the rest will follow. But for now only Christ has been raised and he is ruling the world (v. 25), bringing it closer to God's final plans, no matter what the opposition.

Why is it so important to Paul that Christ has been raised?

What difference does it make to know that Christ is bringing the world under his reign?

Galatians 5:13-26 The fruit of the Spirit

In the Old Testament, God's people were bound to keep his commands by law, but their hearts (or what Paul calls their 'sinful nature') often remained disobedient. Under the new covenant, God calls us to keep in step with his Spirit, who naturally develops goodness in our lives.

How would you sum up the life of the Spirit Paul writes about here?

What fruit of the Spirit (v. 22-23) is God seeking to grow in you at the moment? How can you cooperate with this?

Ephesians 1:15-2:10 The power of the resurrection

The driving force behind Paul's mammoth sentences here is the mighty fact of the resurrection. The resurrection gives us hope (v. 18), demonstrates the power available to us (v. 19-21) and reassures us that Jesus reigns on our behalf (v. 22-23). But, amazingly, not just Christ was raised. Everyone who is 'in Christ', who responds to his call, has also been raised (2:6). We may not have died yet, but spiritually speaking there's a sense in which we are already with God in heaven.

Look over the passage again. What is there here to thank God for?

Philippians 2:1-11 The humble king

Humility isn't just a nice Christian virtue – it's essential currency in the kingdom of God. There's something deeply humble about God himself, and there's no better picture of this than Jesus Christ. It's this that inspires Paul himself to surrender all his privileges ('I consider everything a loss compared to the surpassing greatness of knowing Christ Jesus my Lord, for whose sake I have lost all things. I consider them garbage, that I may gain Christ' 3:8).

Why do we find it so hard to be servants to those around us?

Which of these verses speaks to you?

Colossians 3:12-17 Life together in the body of Christ

Believers in Jesus aren't isolated individuals. We are bound together as 'members of one body' and called to display the truth about God by the way we love each other (v. 15). Any community that tries to live up to this calling will need exactly what Paul recommends here: plenty of forgiveness and love, a thankful spirit and the life-giving message of Jesus.

What should be the marks of our life together?

What keeps you from doing this with Christians around you?

1 John 4:7-21 God's love in us

Being a Christian is more than a set of beliefs, more even than having God living in us – it's actually to live in God (v. 16)! Somehow this means being so close to him that his plans gradually become our plans, and his character ours. God the Father, Son and Holy Spirit live in a continual relationship of love. To be a Christian is to join the mystery of God's love.

What strikes you from John's words?

Resurrection and the Church: Group Discussion

Study Passage: Ephesians 1:15-2:10

What strikes you from this passage?

According to this passage, what can happen now Christ has been raised?

What kind of new life is Paul expecting in the people of God?

How do the truths of this passage connect with your life?

Questions for Reflection

How has God been speaking to you about himself and the Big Story?

What has challenged or inspired you?

The seventh episode of the Big Story concerns the formation of a community of love, moving in the power of the Spirit, taking Christ's message to the world.
How can you see these themes playing out in your life?

Episode 8
The New Creation
REVELATION 21-22

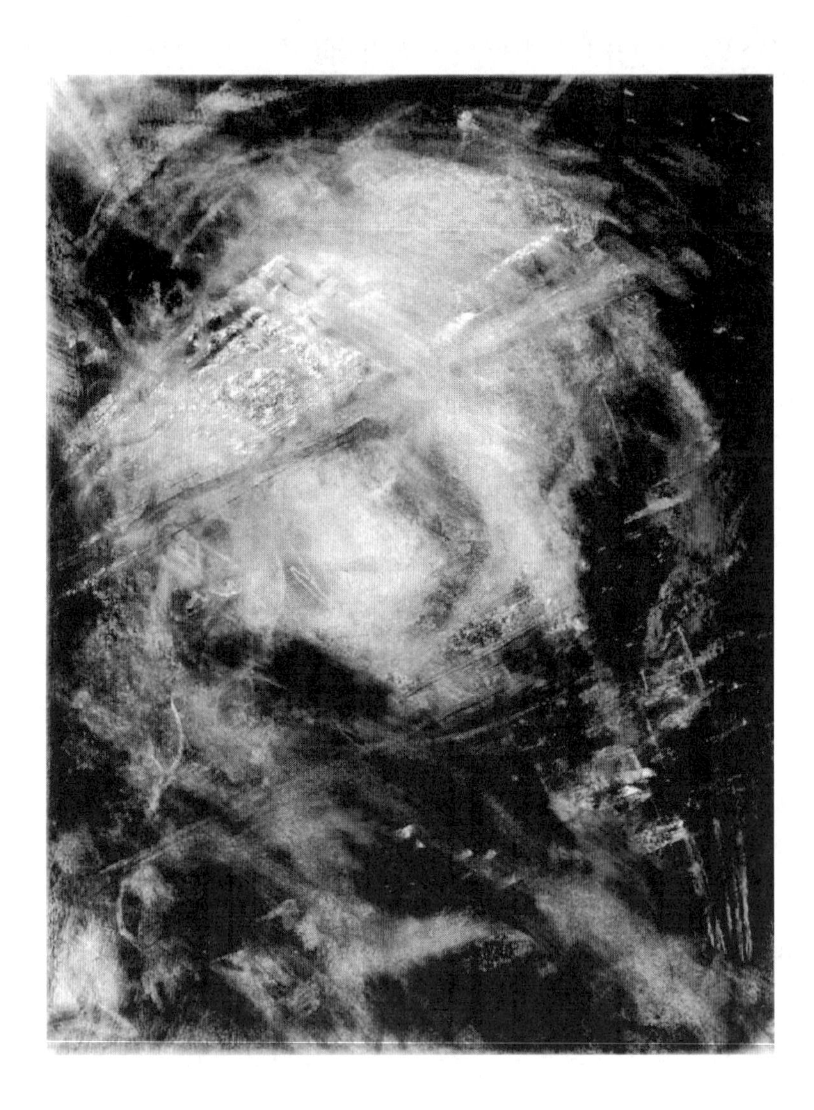

Overview

The ending of our story - the story of God, his people and the world - is too wonderful for words. It is too distant to be seen, too wild to predict and yet it is already in motion and could finally arrive at any moment. We began with creation; we end with new creation. The universe God made will one day be set to rights and bought to perfection. And his people will live with him in future ages that will unfold without ceasing.

Evil will not triumph, death will not remain,
God will complete his new creation

Many Christians are discouraged from thinking about the new creation. It seems like fantasy, a cause of arguments or bizarre ideas, or maybe it just feels a million miles from the daily reality we see around us. It's true that Revelation, the New Testament book devoted to the last things, is full of pictures and symbols (see Revelation chapters 4-22). Some of these are intended to inspire faithfulness in suffering, not to give precise predictions. But the entire Bible looks forward to a time of fulfilment - a future so certain it can be expected, trusted and banked on, even though it's hard for us to imagine. This is what has sustained believers through terrible trials, and it challenges us today to look beyond our own lives to what God is planning.

The bedrock certainty of God's future is resurrection. Jesus died and was raised, therefore anyone who belongs to him will rise like him to spend eternity with God. But before this finally takes place, there must be an end. Evil will not triumph, death will not remain, injustice will be righted, humanity cannot go its wicked way forever. God will intervene in this world's history to bring an end to suffering and evil, and to complete the new creation begun in Jesus Christ. At this point everyone who has ever lived will be raised to face judgement. Each person will face the truth of their life and what they have done with what they were given. Those who have turned away from God and rejected his grace will be punished with eternal separation from him. Those who have accepted God's grace will be saved, and if they have invested much in God's kingdom they will be richly rewarded. Then the new creation will begin in its fullness: a new world, creation healed, a new journey of the wonder of God and the very best that human life promises enjoyed to the full.

Until that awesome day the challenge and the promise remain. The challenge to use every opportunity to follow God and to share the good news of his grace in Jesus. And the promise that he is with us, he is coming, there is always hope and nothing done in Jesus' name is ever wasted.

Key Passages

OLD TESTAMENT LINKS

Isaiah 65:17-25 New heavens and a new earth

After the exile, Israel's world felt small and desperate. At that time these words from the last part of Isaiah spoke of God's plans for Jerusalem, the world and the whole universe! Some of these promises were fulfilled after the exile, or in the miraculous ministry of Jesus, when God's future rushed forwards to meet us in the present. But many promises and pictures still remain for when God finally sets creation to rights.

What parts of this passage appeal to you?

What can we do to bring some of these hopes to reality around our world as signs of the king's coming?

NEW TESTAMENT LINKS

Matthew 19:16-30 Living for future reward

Jesus fully expected a great reversal when what he called 'the renewal of all things' arrived (v. 28). But that reversal also starts here and now – the rich man goes away empty, but those who leave their old life to follow Jesus find lasting treasure.

How can we live in light of the fact that the great reversal is coming?

Mark 13:1-31 Judgement soon and later

Here, 40 years before it happened in 70AD, Jesus accurately predicts the destruction of the Jerusalem Temple (v. 1-4). Roman soldiers would desecrate the Temple (v. 14), the disciples would flee, and all within one generation of Jesus himself. But this passage works on two levels. Also in view is the final triumph of Jesus, the Son of Man, and so some of the warnings and promises still stand for us today.

Which of these warnings have been fulfilled since Jesus spoke them?

What attitude is Jesus looking for in his followers?

Matthew 24:36-51 Parables of judgement

Amazingly, Jesus admits that even he doesn't know when the end will come. Predicting dates is not important. What matters is being watchful and faithful. We should never forget that judgement day will be a day of great surprises (see 25:31-46).

Do you ever think about the fact that Jesus could come tomorrow?

What does it mean to be a 'faithful and wise servant' (v. 45)?

🚌 Romans 8:18-39 Creation will be released

God's plan isn't to wipe out the universe forever and send our spirits to heaven. God intends to redeem our bodies (to resurrect them) so we can live in a renewed universe. Creation itself waits for this destiny. Now Christians have 'the firstfruits' (v. 23) – a taste of the glorious coming reality and a guarantee that nothing can keep us from God's love.

What things in this passage will help you to wait 'patiently' (v. 25) for the new creation?

1 Corinthians 3:1-17 The day will reveal

Paul was unimpressed by the hero-worship at Corinth. What counts for leaders isn't their place in the opinions of others but their effect on the lives of those they serve. 'The Day' of judgement will bring all this to

light (v. 13). Paul implies here that some ineffective Christians will be saved, but without much to show for it (v. 15).
What would it mean for you to build your faith (and other people's) with costly materials?

Philippians 3:12-4:1 Two ways to live
Paul seeks to inspire the Philippians with his own example. They can follow him, straining towards Jesus, or they can lose themselves in the pursuits of the world around them. What drives Paul, though, is the wild hope of a glorious resurrection body and the dreadful conviction that godless living leads to destruction.
What keeps people in our culture from following Jesus?

What inspiration and example can you draw from Paul?

Colossians 1:15-20 All things
This wondrous poem (possibly an early Christian hymn) tells the story of the world from beginning to end – and the key to it all is Jesus. He was there at the start, giving a reason and a shape to everything; he stepped

into the middle of history to save us; and he is working to bring everything together in the end.

Spend time chewing on the words of this passage and making them your own.

If all things have a place in God's plan, and every detail of our lives can serve his purposes (Colossians 3:23), what difference might this make to the daily business of your life?

1 Thessalonians 4:13-5:11 Lives of hope

For Christians, incredible though it may sound, death is like sleep. We go to be with the Lord and to wait for judgement day and the resurrection (v. 16). So instead of grieving endlessly, we can expect to meet believers who have died when the day comes to celebrate the Lord's coming (it's this kind of cosmic celebration that Paul pictures in verse 17). And instead of living hopelessly, we should live light-filled lives in a dark world, as if the new creation has already dawned.

How does having no hope affect people's lives?

How does this passage encourage you?

2 Peter 3:1-13 God's patience

It can be hard to believe that God will come to wrap up all history. But, as Peter points out, the universe must have come from somewhere; and if God can make it, he can remake it (v. 5-7). Peter sees judgement as a great fire (v. 10). It will lay bare everything in this current world order, but it will also transform it into something wonderfully new (v. 13).

What makes it hard to expect the new creation to finally come?

What should we be doing in the time that remains?

Revelation 1:4-18 The alpha and the omega

John has a vision of God similar to that received by the Old Testament prophets, and inspired by their words (e.g., Ezekiel 1 and Daniel 7:13-14). But the central figure in this vision is Jesus Christ, the key to all God's promises.

Let John's vision stir your imagination. What does it reveal about Jesus Christ?

Revelation 12 Trials and Tribulations

This vision speaks about the life of Jesus and its aftermath (see v. 5). But it powerfully retells his story to draw out the great spiritual battle that went on at that time. The woman probably symbolises God's people (hence 12 stars for 12 tribes / 12 apostles – v. 1). She faces great peril, like John's readers, but as the story unfolds she is helped by God at every point. John emphasizes the harsh reality of evil and persecution, but also that it is futile and temporary.

Imagine hearing this vision as an early Christian enduring extreme persecution. How would it encourage you?

In what ways are you sometimes tempted to give up on the Christian life?

🚌 Revelation 21:1-8, 22-27 The new creation

John's final vision is a mixture of solid promises (the end of pain and evil) and imaginative pictures. The sea, which stands for chaos, is banished, but everything good has a place in God's new world, including believers from every nation.

What strikes you from this awesome vision?

What good aspects of creation are redeemed and transformed in John's vision?

Revelation 22:7-21 The End

Jesus is the centre of The Big Story – the fulfilment of Israel's hopes, the turning point of history and the key to creation's destiny. Even at the very end of the Bible, through him, God's arms are open to all who will say, 'Amen. Come, Lord Jesus.'

What encourages you from these awesome last words?

The New Creation: Group Discussion

Study Passage: Revelation 21:1-8 & 22-27

What strikes you from this passage?

How does John's vision complete the themes of the Big Story?

What do people hope for in today's culture? How does this compare?

What difference does it make to live with this reality in mind?

Questions for Reflection

How has God been speaking to you about himself and the Big Story?

What has challenged or inspired you?

The final episode of the Big Story is about the wonder and promise of all that God has planned; it also concerns the hope and perseverance that should mark our lives in the meantime.
How can you see these themes playing out in your life?

The Whole Bible in 66 Sentences
Bible FAQs
Further Reading

EXTRA

EXTRA: The Whole Bible in 66 Sentences

THE OLD TESTAMENT

The Law

The first 5 books of the Old Testament are often called the Law or the Book of Moses.

Genesis Creation, the fall and the flood, followed by the family lines of Abraham, Isaac and Jacob
Exodus The escape from Egypt and the giving of the law through Moses
Leviticus A collection of the laws of Israel
Numbers Life in the wilderness, the people's rebellion and more laws
Deuteronomy Moses' farewell speech – encouragement to be faithful and warnings for disobedience

Old Testament History

There are two separate streams of history in the Old Testament. Joshua to 2 Kings picks up from Deuteronomy and tells the history of Israel, especially from the perspective of the northern kingdom. 1 Chronicles to Esther takes most of the same period and retells the story from the perspective of Judah, including the events of the exile.

Joshua The conquest of the promised land by Joshua and the 12 tribes
Judges Judges like Deborah, Gideon and Samson deliver Israel from oppression
Ruth One woman's faithfulness earns her a place in King David's family tree
1 Samuel Samuel anoints Saul as King of Israel and then David as his replacement
2 Samuel David brings peace and prosperity to Israel, despite personal sin and family rebellion
1 Kings Solomon builds his Temple, then the kingdom splits and Israel's evil kings are opposed by Elijah
2 Kings The last kings: despite prophets like Elisha and Isaiah, Israel is invaded and then Judah is exiled

1 Chronicles A parallel account of David's reign in all its glory
2 Chronicles From Solomon, through the kings –good and bad – to Judah's exile and return
Ezra Ezra's account of his return to bring holiness and God's law to Israel
Nehemiah Nehemiah recounts the rebuilding of Jerusalem's wall and the purifying of God's people
Esther Bold Queen Esther saves the Jews from destruction at the hands of the Persian Empire

Poetry & Wisdom

These books were collected as works of literature or, like psalms and proverbs, they record the ongoing worship and teaching given in Israel from the time of the early kings.

Job A poetic debate between a righteous man who suffers and his opponents, which is eventually settled by God
Psalms 150 songs which praise God, express sorrow, pray for help and tell Israel's story
Proverbs The value of wisdom and a large collection of wise sayings
Ecclesiastes Reflections on the meaninglessness of many things and the need for perspective in life
Song of Songs A sensual poem celebrating desire, love and sex

The Prophets

The four Major Prophets come first (along with Lamentations). Isaiah lived before the exile (though the words in later chapters relate to the exile and afterwards). Jeremiah spoke as the exile took place. Ezekiel had already been exiled to Babylon with Israel's nobility. Babylon is also the setting for the stories and prophecies of Daniel.

The twelve Minor Prophets are roughly grouped according to time scale. Most of the first six concern the fall of the northern kingdom and early threats to Judah in the south. The next three may reflect the southern kingdom's impending invasion by Babylon, and the last three relate to the return from exile.

Isaiah Judgement for Israel and the nations, then comfort for the exiles and a cosmic vision of the future

Jeremiah Despite opposition, Jeremiah predicts the exile but also foresees a new covenant
Lamentations A brief lament for the fall of Jerusalem and prayers for restoration
Ezekiel God will judge all nations and Israel's corrupt leaders, but he plans to renew Israel by his Spirit
Daniel Daniel is protected in exile and given dreams of God's coming kingdom

Hosea God, Israel's loving husband, warns the unfaithful northern kingdom to repent or face destruction
Joel An unknown prophet urges repentance before the LORD comes both to judge and to save
Amos Northern Israel's unjust society proves that her worship is meaningless and she is ready for judgement
Obadiah God's enemies in Edom should not gloat: his people may suffer, but they will be restored
Jonah Jonah's disobedience and hard-heartedness is a parable for self-centred Israel
Micah Judah must trust in God, not armies or idols, but one day the nations will come to God through Israel

Nahum Mighty Nineveh will fall, but Israel will somehow be restored
Habakkuk Habakkuk complains about judgement for Judah, but learns to trust in God's deliverance
Zephaniah God will flatten Judah and other proud nations but one day he will rejoice over his people

Haggai Back from exile, God's people should concentrate on completing the new temple
Zechariah God's returned people need to be cleansed and trust in the awesome future he will bring
Malachi God will return to Israel again, but her priests and people must be holy

THE NEW TESTAMENT

New Testament History

The gospels each tell the story of Jesus, often including the same events, but each telling the story in their own way to give us a fuller picture of Jesus' life, death and resurrection. The book of Acts continues from Luke's gospel with the story of the early church.

Matthew Jesus is Israel's Messiah, her greatest teacher and healer, and the fulfilment of all prophecy
Mark Jesus announces God's kingdom and calls disciples to follow him whatever the cost
Luke In the power of the Spirit, Jesus brings good news to the poor and salvation to all the world
John Jesus, God's only Son, calls Israel to believe in him and enter into the life he brings

Acts Luke's account of the spread of the church, the inclusion of Gentiles and Paul's ministry

The Letters

The New Testament includes 13 letters written to churches or individuals connected with Paul, and also letters written by the author of Hebrews (whose identity we don't know!), James, Peter, John and Jude.

Romans Paul's great exposition of salvation and the place of Israel in God's plan for the world
1 Corinthians Paul appeals for less chaos and more loving concern at Corinth
2 Corinthians Paul defends his apostleship, despite its weak and troubled appearance
Galatians A stern warning to trust in Christ and live by the Spirit rather than seeking to be circumcised
Ephesians God has created a new humanity in Christ, raised with him to live a new life in the Spirit
Philippians Paul joyfully encourages humility, living for Christ alone and a lifestyle of contentment
Colossians Very like Ephesians, but also warning against false religions and philosophies

1 Thessalonians Encouragement to go on pleasing God and waiting for Jesus to bring the resurrection
2 Thessalonians The need to stand firm amidst global chaos and the coming judgement
1 Timothy Timothy should bring order in Ephesus and warn against false teaching
2 Timothy Timothy must be faithful and finish his race despite difficult circumstances
Titus Titus is to appoint faithful leaders on Crete and encourage godly living in the world
Philemon Paul urges Philemon to accept a runaway slave back into his household

Hebrews Encouragement to keep going and focus on Jesus, who fulfils the Old Testament

James A challenge to live righteously and unselfishly at a time of suffering and need
1 Peter The church is the people of God, built on Christ to live holy lives in difficult times
2 Peter God's word can be trusted and his judgement will come

1 John True believers are marked by holy living, assurance of forgiveness, belief in Christ and selfless love
2 John Encouragement to love and to avoid false teaching
3 John Brief greetings, commendations and encouragements

Jude Avoiding immorality, and persevering in a dark age

New Testament Prophecy

Revelation is in a category of its own. Part letter, part prophecy, it addresses the persecution of the church at the time, but also gives hope for the future.

Revelation The risen Christ speaks to his church, conquers Satan and brings final judgement and the new creation

EXTRA: Bible FAQs

Which Bible version is best?

There is no perfect version of the Bible. The main difference is whether they seek to stick closely to the original languages, or whether they prioritise being easier to follow. Translations like the New Revised Standard Version, New American Standard Bible and English Standard Version strive for an accurate translation. Others, like the New International Version (or Today's New International Version) and New Century Version try to strike a balance. Versions such as the New Living Translation, Good News Bible and The Message are more paraphrases than actual translations. The key is to use a Bible you find it helpful to engage with, and to check multiple translations if ever you are in doubt.

When was the Bible written?

Most of the Old Testament seems to have been finally compiled after the exile in the 4th Century BC. This explains some of the signs of editing and the theological hindsight it displays. But the sources for the final form of the books are much earlier, in copies of the law (e.g., Joshua 24:26), royal annals (e.g., 1 Kings 11:41), official records (e.g., Ruth 4:10), previous histories (e.g., Joshua 10:13) and traditional genealogies (e.g., Exodus 6:16). Some Old Testament material has a clear and direct link with those who wrote it (like the scrolls of Jeremiah - Jeremiah 36); other early material represents traditions that had been safeguarded and cherished through generations.

The New Testament was written much closer to the events it describes, with the letters being written between 55 and 90 AD and the gospels (probably Mark first) produced in the same time window.

Do today's Bibles contain what was originally written?

To a high degree of certainty, yes. Jewish scribes had a reputation for painstaking accuracy and recent discoveries (for instance, a 2nd Century BC copy of Isaiah found among the Dead Sea Scrolls in

1947) confirm that the many copies we have of the Hebrew Scriptures have remained essentially unchanged over the centuries.

Modern New Testament translations are based on over 5,000 early manuscripts, some from the 2nd and 3rd Centuries AD. Cross-referencing this magnitude of copies from so many different sources allows us to be very confident that we can get back to the original source. This discipline (known as textual criticism) isn't perfect, but it is highly accurate.

Can we trust the Bible?

It's worth bearing in mind that Scripture hasn't been complied like a dusty police statement – it's a living, creative witness put together in various genres by many different writers. Its purpose has always been to engage hearts, minds and lives, not to be a science textbook or knockdown historical proof of God. But it is a truly reliable book.

The Bible is packed with historical, geographical and archeological details many of which have been independently verified. It was transmitted and written by individuals and communities who witnessed the events they described. These events (like the exile or the miracles of Jesus) profoundly shaped those passing on their story, so there was little risk of details being forgotten, and little point in stories being fabricated. The Bible is pervaded by the value of integrity and the rejection of false witness. Its contents have been handed down with great care and at great cost.

Even if some events in scripture are difficult to place historically or impossible to verify, the key to scripture's trustworthiness is the life, death and resurrection of Jesus, for which we have some of the strongest evidence. If these events took place, as there is good reason to suppose, they demonstrate that supernatural events *do* occur in history, and that the God behind the story of scripture is faithful to his word. If this is the case, a trustful approach to the witness of scripture is the best one to take.

How were the Bible books selected? Were some books missed out?

The scriptures we have are just some of the records God's people have kept, and a small proportion of the sacred literature generated over many centuries. The difference, however, is that in each case there has been an overwhelming sense, proven over time, that God speaks through these particular books. It was only natural for Jews and early Christians who were identifying a 'canon' or list of inspired books to turn to works known to be by people such as Isaiah, Ezra, Paul, Luke and John. These books are by far the most accurate and well attested, the closest to the significant events in the history of salvation, and they speak with a voice beyond the capabilities of the original writer.

There are some Jewish religious works from between the Testaments (such as the Apocrypha) not covered in this guide. There are also late, sub-Christian documents (such as the 'gospel of Thomas') which some have claimed give a more reliable picture than the four gospels we have. This is highly unlikely as they were written later (possibly centuries later) and in a different culture, by people who had no link to the initial disciples and who were clearly influenced more by Greek philosophy than first century Palestinian Judaism or the teachings of Jesus.

What about difficult bits in the Bible?

God speaks clearly through the scriptures when we listen obediently and interpret the words carefully together. But this is no guarantee that we will understand every verse in its fullness.

There are parts of scripture we remain unsure of, despite centuries of consideration. Some sections are much disputed. But the main teachings of scripture are perfectly (even uncomfortably) clear. One thing to bear in mind with difficult parts of the Bible is that the Big Story of scripture unfolds gradually, and amidst the brokenness of a fallen world. As a general rule, we should judge God not on the worst excesses of tribal violence in the book of the Judges, but on the depth of love and wisdom in the life of Jesus Christ. He alone is the key to the whole story – as long as we keep his life and teachings central, the rest will somehow fall into place.

EXTRA: Further Reading

How to Read the Bible for all it's Worth, Fee & Stewart (Zondervan 2003)

Wise, scholarly and practical help with reading the various genres in scripture. Easy to get into and well worth the investment.

The New Bible Commentary (IVP 1994)

A very useful one-volume Bible commentary, with sufficient detail on each passage to answer many of the questions raised by the text.

The Lion Handbook (Lion Hudson 2002)

A classic, best-selling, well-illustrated basic bible guide.

A Walk through the Bible, Lesslie Newbigin (Triangle 1999)

This short book is a brilliant summary of the whole sweep of the Bible, given in a talk by a great theologian. This guide owes a great deal to his insights.

The Spectacular Ordinary Life, Viv Thomas (Authentic Lifestyle 2008)

A practical and inspiring guide to living in God's story in our daily lives.

The Book of God *and* Paul: a Novel, Walter Wangerin (Lion 1996, 2000)

Two wonderful novels telling the Bible story in vivid and moving detail – read them to get a real flavour for the great characters in God's story.

The Challenge of Jesus, N T Wright (SPCK 2000)

A new look at Jesus, his message, and the history of God's people by a leading New Testament scholar. Full of fresh insights for those who want to think more deeply about God's story and another big influence on this guide.

Also by Mark Powley

READ ON FOR EXCERPT . . .

Changing Values

In October 1947 pilot Chuck Yeager was pushing the Bell X-1 jet faster and faster in his attempt to be the first human to break the sound barrier. The closer he got, though, the more G-Force there was and the more the plane would shake. In fact, after a certain point, the controls would fail altogether.

Changing our values is like breaking through the sound barrier. The driving forces behind our life have a hidden power, holding us back from the life God calls us to. The approval we long for from our workmates, the intimacy we crave from immoral sex, our fear of conflict, or desperate desire to prove ourselves - these forces cause our lives to shudder as we start to change.

Before the barriers are broken, before God takes his rightful place in our lives, we must confront the values we hold most dear. 'What's wrong with you?', others might say; or 'Don't you love me?'; or 'You're taking this too seriously'. Other opposition will come from within. You may find that you're struggling to even *want* to change, and the doubts and problems seem to be getting worse. This is because in your heart of hearts other values still reign over God's values.

The struggle is a sign of hope, though. It shows that your values are shifting and your world is being slowly transformed. Chuck Yeager did break the sound barrier eventually. The risk was worth it. What about you?

The Cost of God's Values

Which priorities must take second place?
Luke 14:25-27

What else must we give up?
Luke 14:33

How did Paul's values change?
Philippians 3:7-8

Jesus wasn't contradicting the greatest commandments here - we're not to be hateful towards our families. But he knows what our key values often are: loved ones, our own safety, our possessions. If God's will is going to come first in our lives, there will be a conflict with the other values. When it comes down to a choice, it will be *as if* we hate them. This was Paul's experience. Many things in his life had been valuable, but 'compared to...knowing Christ Jesus' he was willing to *consider* them rubbish. Some of the values that drive us are healthy, others aren't so healthy, but none of them deserve the prime place that belongs to God.

Changing My Values

Like a home make-over programme, the Christian life is about letting a designer loose in your most treasured inner rooms. There's a risk (safari-style wallpaper) but also a benefit (the home of your dreams). But no make-over can happen without losing the old furniture and decoration.

Don't underestimate the pain of this process. It means giving up our secret love affair with the many things that take God's place in our lives. It means learning to surrender - to give God the keys to each part of our lives and let him go to work. 'The reason many are still troubled, still seeking, still making little forward progress', wrote A. W. Tozer, 'is because they haven't come to the end of themselves. We're still trying to give orders, and interfering with God's work in us'.

It's also tempting to simply pretend that our values have changed: to tick the right boxes and say that God is N° 1. It's better to be honest, though, and in the end, the pain is worth it. God's ambitious plans for us are way beyond our feeble imagination. As C. S. Lewis once wrote, 'You thought you were going to be made into a decent little cottage, but he is building a palace. He intends to come and live in it himself'.

Return to your values list (Values 6). Look at the high values. Think of examples of how they affect your actions.

What would you like your top values to be?

What will stop you changing your values?

Time to Change

When we were baptised, we died to the values of this world and came alive to God's values. But your baptism needs to be daily renewed in your life. In particular, there will come a time when your decision for Christ will be tested. You will face a battle of values. Another Christian will hurt you deeply, or you'll face unexpected suffering. A seductive temptation will hunt you down, or you'll gradually realise that you're drifting away from God. At that time, your values will be tested to the core. This is why Jesus calls us to make our choice for him now, before the time of testing comes.

Meanwhile, the process of changing values and developing godly habits will take many years. But don't be discouraged. As one writer says, 'to be changed into the person God wants us to be will take a lifetime. But by happy coincidence, that is precisely how much time each one of us has been given'.

⌛ Closer to God

Look over the Values material and make notes over the page for the Values meeting.

Try to commit the memory verse (p. 35) to your mind.

Cell UK Resources

4Life
Mark Powley
Contributions from Liz West and Trevor Withers
4Life is an introduction to a different way of living, as a disciple of Jesus Christ. Like all the best journeys this book will leave you changed by the time you finish. It's written with spaces for you to record your reactions as you go through it. 4Life has been developed for new Christians or anyone seeking to refresh their faith and go deeper with God. It is full of honesty, passion and humour, and seeks to give a solid foundation for practical Christian living in the worldwide church of God.

4Life Group Notes
Mark Powley
4Life Group Notes are written to be used alongside '4Life' which was originally written to be used in four 1-to-1 meetings with another Christian. These Group Notes make the same material accessible to small groups over a 10-week/10-session course (technically it should be renamed 10Life!).

Walking Together
Liz West and Trevor Withers
This booklet looks at lessons we can learn from the way Jesus worked with His disciples and how the Early church understood discipleship. It outlines ways that we can both become and make effective disciples in our 21st century culture, using current metaphors and hands-on material. It is focused on one-to-one relationships that need to be in place for good spiritual formation to occur.

Walking with Jesus
Gary Gibbs
Designed for new Christians, each section is packed with principles by which to live. The interactive style not only helps to apply the ideas, but also gives energy and confidence to use them. This book will help the reader more clearly define God's plan for their life.

Sowing Reaping Keeping
Laurence Singlehurst
The Christian gospel is the best story ever told. Yet many of those who hear it perceive it as a threat. Laurence Singlehurst believes that much of the threat would be removed if Christians would respect and understand the people they are approaching. This short, crisp and often humorous book is full of seeds of wisdom for those who long to make permanent disciples for Jesus. Discover the reasons why evangelism may have been difficult in the past and learn new ideas to help you share your faith in a relevant way.

12.5 Steps to Spiritual Health
Howard Astin
This is a powerful course for new Christians and mature believers alike, designed to clear the rubbish out of our lives and help us grow towards spiritual maturity. Howard takes us through each of the steps and gives instructions at the end of each chapter to enable us to move forward and deal with the issues that will surface. Our promise is freedom in Christ. 12.5 Steps to Spiritual Health is a valuable tool to help us make this promise a reality.

Loving the Lost
Laurence Singlehurst
The journey guide is a review tool to help us understand where we are on our Christian journey. A Journey Guide for Growing Christians and A Journey Guide for New Believers are invaluable as people grow in their faith and move towards leadership. They are laid out in an easy to use format and are designed to be reviewed with a sponsor.

Simply Cell
Laurence Singlehurst, Liz West and Trevor Withers
What it stays on the cover is what this book is about. It explains cell in a dynamic yet simple way. Suitable for anyone about to join a cell whether they are from Alpha or existing church members who are new to cell. This booklet will also encourage long-term cell people.

Cell UK Resources

Cell UK is committed to supporting local churches in both mission and discipleship through the development of small groups often called cells. These groups are always connected to and work with the larger expressions of church.

We work with most major denominations and new church streams offering published resources, training conferences and a regular magazine.

Our heart is to see the great commandment fulfilled through people loving God, loving one another and loving our world.

Cell UK also offer a range of training opportunities and conferences. For current information browse our website at:
www.celluk.org.uk

About the Author

Mark Powley

Mark is married to Ailsa and has three boys, Jonah, Zach and Nathan. He has been a theology student, secondary school teacher and curate, and he is now an Associate Pastor at St. Paul's Hammersmith. Mark is a founding friend of Breathe, a Christian network for simpler living (www.ibreathe.org.uk).

The Artist, Rydal Hanbury

Rydal studied her BA in Fine Art at the University of Hertfordshire, winning the University Award in 1999 & 2004. She completed the Drawing Year 2008. Rydal won 1st Prize in "Hung, Drawn and Quartered"; her drawing was converted into a 75ft hoarding covering part of the Tower of London, for a 3 year Restoration Project. She is interested in drawing as a means of 'capturing the present moment in time' within a defined area. Its containment, claustrophobic and repetitive aspects, patterns and rhythms. She is at present working on drawings on the Square Mile around the City of London. These drawings can be seen on her website.